Endorsements

Life isn't always easy. Sometimes it's just plain impossible, filled with physical and verbal abuse, pain, betrayals and family relational disasters. These things create rejection, inability to trust, depression, grief and hopelessness, and a view of the world as a dangerous place to be because of the people who live there. People experiencing such relational disasters are damaged, marred, in pain and don't know how to get out of this dark, dangerous world.

Yet miracles do happen because we have a God who is first and foremost a Father, yet God. God loves people, adores us and longs to change our story, creating a whole new history in our lives. This book is a testimony of how the outrageous love of Jesus found an abused and rejected young woman longing for family, wholeness and life. Belma has written her story—one that will touch many caught in the web of hurt and pain. This book is touching; it will make you cry. It is healing, pouring the oil of love into raw bleeding wounds. It will create a future and expectations for those who have given up.

For those like me who've already been healed, it's another amazing example of the absolutely outrageous love of Jesus reaching out to those captured in pain and hopelessness. Get this book not only for yourself, but buy copies for your friends who are captured in back dark alleys of pain and despair. It may just save their life. This is real!

BARBARA J. YODER
Lead apostle, Shekinah Regional Apostolic Center
Author, international speaker

What a story! Belma captured my heart the whole way through. Her book should be turned into a m  as transformed many of our lives. Looking ful woman. You would never know the jou e story inspires me to see how the King o akes all things beautiful.

I recently had the chance to talk to Belma and one of her phrases jumped out to me. She said, "Stuff just doesn't matter. I only want space to dance before the Lord." I see in her heart's cry and in her life the passion of Isaiah 61:1 and 3. I thank Belma for taking me on a journey of her life. It challenges me to keep going.

STEVE AND SANDRA LONG
Vice presidents, Catch the Fire
Senior leaders, Catch the Fire Toronto
Authors, international speakers

One of the things that so impacted me with Belma's story is her incredible passion and persistence to live, overcome loss and rejection, and discover who she really is. The Belma Vardy I know today is a miracle of restoration—a carrier of joy, immense integrity, and purpose as she fulfills her destiny with a hugely thankful heart. She has been given beauty for ashes, the oil of joy for mourning, and a garment of praise instead of a spirit of heaviness. This down-to-earth book brings hope, encouragement and fresh vision to readers who need their hearts and emotions healed from the pains and abuses of life.

MARY AUDREY RAYCROFT
Pastor, teacher, author and international speaker

"In this world you will have trouble," Jesus said. "But take heart! I have overcome the world" (John 16:33, NIV). For some, that forecast of "trouble" is tragic. *"But God!"* How I treasure those two words found throughout the Bible, assuring us of a bigger story, being written by the One who is always able to redeem whatever life throws at us. It has been said that "trials are designed to develop our trust muscles." No wonder Belma is living and sharing such a dynamic faith adventure!

Because God Was There will give you fascinating personal glimpses into dramatic events in world history and take you deep into the spiritual realm where healing, wholeness and a life of purpose are always waiting in the restorative embrace of our loving Saviour. This book should be in every counsellor's office.

MOIRA BROWN
Author, Canadian television and radio personality
More than 40 years of broadcast experience, including co-host of 100 Huntley Street
Named one of Canada's top 100 Christian women leaders

Belma Vardy's book demonstrates God's mercy and grace upon her life. The experience of being rejected by her mother, being disconnected from her father, and later being torn from her grandparents should be an encouragement and inspiration to all who read her story.

PASTOR JOSEPH GILBERT
Senior pastor, Walpole Island Evangelistic Centre
Served on Walpole Island Council of Three Fires, 18 years
Former Chief, 12 years, Walpole Island

This book you have in front of you is more than just a story or a testimony of God's faithfulness, but this book, *Because God Was There* by Belma Vardy, is a manual to lead you from tragedy to triumph and take the *mess-ups* of life and turn them into a *message* of eternal life. You will find yourself tearing up, then rejoicing together with Belma as she turns every tribulation into an opportunity to enter greater levels of the Kingdom. I love the central message in this narrative: Hope! That no matter how hard or impossible the situations of life are, God can take every intended curse and turn it into a wonderful blessing that will more than make up for the evil of any day.

My prayer is that you, through this book, will find the audacity to hope again, even in the midst of your negative situations, and see, once again, the goodness of the Lord in the land of the living.

BARRY C. MARACLE (MOHAWK)
Prophet, pastor and itinerate minister, Desert Stream Ministries

I have known Belma for at least two decades and have always been impressed with how cheerful and full of life she is. But I also know, after reading this book, that she has made some wonderful choices that completely changed the course of her life. In the natural, because of her past, she should be angry, resentful, and very hurt, but God responded to her good choices and brought impossible healing and freedom. All things are possible with God. If He can do it for Belma, He can do it for you no matter how horrific your life may have been. You will be encouraged and blessed reading her life story.

JEREMY SINNOTT, BA, OTC, MA, OPC
Author, pastor, Catch the Fire Barrie
Worship leader and itinerant speaker, retired principal and teacher

My wife, Inger, and I have known Belma for several years. We had no idea her past was so traumatic and hurtful until we read this autobiography. This book is a powerful testimony to the unconditional and enduring love of Father God. While Belma's circumstances were often distressing, her identity was never in doubt...Anyone who reads Belma's story will want to have the same intimacy with the Father that she has!

RALPH A. BEISNER
Author, pastor, The Father's Paradigm Ministry, Hyde Park, NY
Retired New York State Supreme Court Justice
East Coast Coordinator for Partners in Harvest

You will be forever changed upon reading *Because God Was There*. It is a riveting and heart-wrenching story of hardships, grief, pain and the unfairness of some of life's most horrendous circumstances. Yet it also speaks of grace, faith, resilience, redemption, and the abiding love of Yeshua (Jesus), the tribal man who saves, wraps, and seals us in His unending love.

This book is a devotional and catalyst to the healing process in the reader's own life. With a Discussion and Study Guide, along with Pause and Reflect sections, individuals will benefit from this resource as a launching pad to a journey of healing for congregations, small groups and personal settings.

We have known Belma for years. To meet her you would never know the extent of the pain and suffering she has had to endure. Loving, kind, generous, gracious—she is truly a remarkable woman and a dancing miracle, a lady of honour and dignity we are proud to call our sister and friend. To all our relations: this book can help bring healing to our people, especially "Indian" residential/boarding school "survivors." *Because God Was There* is a must-read for every person who has ever experienced trauma or hurts in life.

GERARD (ABOUYOU) ROBERTS, DVM (KARINA)
AND PETA-GAY (TAYALITI) ROBERTS (TAINO/ARAWAK)
International speakers, Worship Keepers
First Nations dancers

I could not put down Belma's book, except to choke back tears so as not to become a puddle in public. Her journey has touched me profoundly, as it will anyone who has experienced even a little of her trauma. Thank you, Belma, for showing us the way into forgiveness, hope—even celebration.

BECKY THOMAS
Foursquare pastor, Saskatoon, SK
Native American Music Award recipient
2011 Best Female Artist

As a young child, Belma Vardy lived through the brutal and terrifying events that accompanied the sudden erection of the Berlin Wall, when east was separated from west and families were ripped apart. Providentially, she was there almost 30 years later to witness and celebrate its destruction. Her gripping personal narrative, as told in *Because God Was There,* is also a journey out of extraordinary abuse and painful separation to a place of restoration, forgiveness, and joy that can only be found in Christ.

Embodied in this transformational story is the encouraging truth that God can use our fractured and broken stories to bring healing and hope to others. It is also a powerful testimony to the role that dance can play when expressed to the glory of the Original Artist.

DR. COLIN HARBINSON
International director of StoneWorks Global Arts Initiative
Author, international conference speaker
Creator and choreographer of Toymaker and Son

BECAUSE GOD WAS THERE

A JOURNEY OF LOSS,
HEALING AND OVERCOMING

BELMA VARDY

Because God Was There. A Journey of Loss, Healing and Overcoming
Copyright ©2017 Crystal Waters Music | belmavardy@celebrationofdance.com
All rights reserved
Printed in Canada
ISBN 978-1-927355-85-5 soft cover
ISBN 978-1-927355-86-2 EPUB

Published by: Castle Quay Books
Tel: (416) 573-3249
E-mail: info@castlequaybooks.com | www.castlequaybooks.com

Edited by Marina Hofman Willard
Portrait photo by Daniel Holmes Photography

Some names in this manuscript have been changed to protect people's privacy.

Foreword by Lorne Shepherd

Library and Archives Canada Cataloguing in Publication

Vardy, Belma, author
    Because God was there : a journey of loss, healing and
overcoming / Belma Vardy.

ISBN 978-1-927355-85-5 (softcover)

    1. Vardy, Belma. 2. Christian biography--Germany.
3. Christian biography--Canada. 4. Dance--Religious aspects--
Christianity. 5. Berlin Wall, Berlin, Germany, 1961-1989.
6. Germany--Biography. I. Title.

BR1725.V37A3 2017   270.092   C2017-901056-5

Acknowledgements

Thank you, John and Marion Franklin of Imago! This book has been an Imago project (www.imago-arts.org) made possible through the generous support of donors. Thank you, precious donors!

Many thanks to Daniel Holmes Photography for the portrait photo.

A very special thank you to Ric and Shirley Riordon for guiding the image that reflects my story.

Thank you to the readers who gave of their time and resources: my dear friend Carolyn King (former elected Chief of the Mississaugas of the New Credit First Nation), Becky Thomas, Moira Brown, Lorne and Doris Shepherd, Sam Cooper, Jaime Fernandes and Mary Audrey Raycroft. Thank you, Cheryl Bear, for your support and friendship.

I also thank Diane Roblin-Lee, Daina Doucet, Faith Baczko and Becky Thomas, who poured their hearts, love and souls into this project.

To two motivated editors—an artisan and refiner, Daina Doucet (Summer Breeze), and gracious and God-inspired Faith Baczko: a very special thank you for your deep commitment and dedication to excellence and loyalty; for all the love and care you poured into this project; and for submitting your talent, experience and passion for a common goal—to expose God's glory! Thank you, dear editors! I praise God for such an amazing team of women!

A big heartfelt thank you to Larry Willard, managing editor Marina Willard and Castle Quay Books. I am grateful for your wisdom, support and oversight of this labour of love in every step of the project.

To God the Father, God the Son and God the Holy Spirit,

Jesus my eternal Bridegroom

All blessing and glory and honour and power forever

I offer this with praise and thanksgiving

For You alone are Worthy.

Contents

Foreword

Belma is the best example I know of someone whose mourning has been turned into dancing and whose sorrow has become praise. She and I met at a wedding. I was the officiant, and Belma was there as an instructor who had brought a group of children she had trained in worship dance to perform during the wedding ceremony. I was impressed. This was not just dance; it was praise and worship. The children were worshipping, and the presence of the Lord was there.

After the wedding Belma came to me for counselling at the Bayridge Family Centre. Her background shaped her present life and her journey as she follows the Lord in ministry, and it has been a joy for me not only to share in her recovery from an abusive childhood but also to observe firsthand the miracle of redemption at work in a shattered life.

Belma's story is one of gripping contrasts. It illustrates how one event, or a single life's circumstance, can impact two individuals who share a similar background in widely divergent ways. The trauma Belma endured in her younger years would have destroyed most people. If they had survived, they would have been severely crippled emotionally. But Belma found the key to healing. Her recovery demonstrates that healing is possible for any broken, wounded, rejected soul.

The sum of Belma's experiences makes her the person she is today—loving, compassionate, outgoing and exuberant in her expression of thanksgiving and love to God through worship dance. Her life's journey will not only bless you but change your life and put the key to healing and freedom in your hands.

It has been a privilege for me to know Belma. I am honoured to contribute to her book, because I know her story will be a blessing to you. I am grateful to the Lord to be given the opportunity to assist, support, encourage and help her compile her testimony. It was a labour of love and reliance on the Lord for both of us and was possible only *because God was there.*

Lorne Shepherd

Rev. Lorne Shepherd is a certified pastoral counsellor by Canada Christian College specializing in marriage and family and a veteran in television broadcasting. Lorne is founder of Bayridge Family Centre and Heart to Heart Marriage and Family Ministry. He is proud of his First Nation's heritage. His mother is part Iroquois and Algonquin. Lorne is author of Love Making His Way, Raising Real Kids in an Unreal World, *and* Sex, Never a Four Letter Word.

Preface

God is a great steward, wasting nothing of our pain. Only God so perfectly designed the life of a little girl who spent her childhood in Germany and her teen years unhappily relocated in a foreign environment under severely abusive conditions, so that she could identify with and relate to the pain of Indigenous people.

In 1993 God gave me the opportunity for compassionate ministry with First Nations People "to comfort those who are in any affliction, with the comfort with which we ourselves are comforted by God" (2 Corinthians 1:4, ESV). Since then, I have developed a deep love for them and their teachings and a desire to see them experience cultural redemption. Their chiefs invited me to share my story and participate in their communities. When I tell my testimony, they relate because many were sent to residential schools away from their loved ones, sometimes into abusive situations. Everything I've experienced has been part of their history.

Some background: In the 1870s the Government of Canada partnered with Anglican, Catholic, United and Presbyterian churches to build and run residential schools for First Nations children. Their goal was to educate and integrate Indigenous people into Canadian society and "kill the Indian in the child," according to one government official.

There were more than 130 federally supported residential schools across Canada. The last one closed in Duck Lake, Saskatchewan, as late as 1996. More than 150,000 children, some as young as four years of age, were required to attend these schools. About 80,000 of them are still alive and share their experiences today.

The children were forcibly removed from their homes and separated from their families. The parents had no choice in the matter, and any who protested the removal of their children faced possible imprisonment. The schools were often such long distances away that families lost contact. Visits were seldom permitted.

In the schools, children were forbidden to speak their native language or practice their culture and were often punished for doing so. They were subjected to sexual and mental abuse as well as severe beatings, and many were required to do hard labour. The quality of food they received was poor: too many reports of mouldy, maggot-infested, rotten food surfaced to be ignored.

Children removed from their homes didn't have a chance to learn parenting skills. Many forgot their native language and traditions. Others adopted the abusive behaviours, continuing the cycle of abuse and trauma from one generation to the next.

These communities and people continue to be in great need of healing. Their pain is reflected in high rates of substance abuse, violence, crime, suicide and imprisonment. Dysfunction marks family life. First Nations children today suffer with post-traumatic stress syndrome as a result of abuse experienced by their grandparents and great-grandparents.

In recent years churches and the federal government have issued various statements of apology to Indigenous people, the most notable of which was Prime Minister Stephen Harper's on June 11, 2008, on behalf of all Canadians for the years of residential school atrocities committed against First Nations people.

While the apologies have been necessary, and are welcome, they have not been able to remove the memories of the outrageous treatment First Nations people endured. The abuses have resulted in deep emotional and psychological damage that has made it extremely difficult for survivors to reengage in normal family, social and professional life.

Hundreds of healing initiatives and projects have been funded through the federal government's Aboriginal Healing Foundation and other organizations, but few truly understand the hearts of First Nations people. It's difficult for Canadians to relate to the suffering of Indigenous people because the residential school experience is foreign to their own.

Among the First Nations there is a deep sadness and grief that breeds hopelessness. According to the chiefs, my story dispels grief because I have crossed the divide from hopelessness to healing. When I tell my story, First Nations people identify with it. The chiefs hope their people will receive healing and freedom through it. Thus the reason for writing this book!

I have learned that, as with any authentic relationship, the key to involvement with First Nations people is respect. It is especially important to develop a relationship with an elder. By developing a relationship with an elder, one learns about their culture and comes to understand what transpired in their communities as a result of colonization and assimilation.

During my years of relationship with First Nations people, I have had the privilege of being connected with pastor, counsellor and elder Lorne Shepherd. Lorne has been consistently involved with my story: he counselled me and became my spiritual father. His comments in the "Pause and Reflect" sections are written from a counsellor's perspective to bring understanding and revelation to various experiences in my story.

Also, I am honoured to have the involvement of pastor and Native American Music Award recipient Becky Thomas in this project. Her contribution of the "Discussion and Study Guide" has enriched and given depth to my story. It motivates people to explore their own hearts and relationships to bring wholeness and healing. She also wrote the questions for "Pause and Reflect," giving readers a chance to consider and apply Lorne's nuggets of wisdom within the context of their own lives and circumstances.

I pray that the eyes of your understanding would be enlightened in reading my story and that God would lead you, as you consider the wisdom Lorne and Becky share, to discover the blessings God has reserved for you.

Belma Vardy

Introduction to
Pause and Reflect and
Discussion and Study Guide

Dear Reader,
While reading Belma's story, you may identify with her experiences. It may open old wounds and trigger painful memories. When such memories surface, we can choose to stuff them back into the dark recesses or dusty attics of our minds or to face them and begin a lengthy cleanup.

Cleaning old wounds can be extremely painful; it takes a brave soul to choose this route. However, in facing the pain we come to understand that a broken heart, like a broken bone, needs to be "reset" to function properly. If we care about our emotional and mental health like we do our physical health, we won't stuff the painful memories back even deeper into the dark places of our minds. We will seek healing for their causes rather than apply a Band-Aid of addictions to mask the festering outward symptoms of our brokenness.

Belma neither hid her pain nor became her own doctor, spending years in self-help groups. Instead, she faced her troubles as she waited on the Great Physician and Wonderful Counsellor to examine her and choose the method of treatment. A good patient, she obeyed His instructions—a habit she continues in other areas of her life. This book is a narrative of how God redeemed and restored her and shaped her life into a masterpiece of great victory and miracles as she focused her worship and devotion on Him.

As you read Belma's story, we invite you to slow down enough to hear and capture God's heart for yourself. Lift your eyes heavenward. Invite your heavenly Father to reset your heart. Find out where He is and what He is doing in your own story. Allow yourself to get "unstuck" from past and present circumstances. Know that you're not alone.

To this end, we provide two resources for you, intended to give you, dear reader, an opportunity to come closer to God, our Healer. "Pause and Reflect" sections at the end of several chapters provide reflections from Lorne Shepherd, a Christian counsellor and Belma's friend, and following the epilogue is a "Discussion and Study Guide." Both resources can be used for personal use or in a small-group setting.

Healing came to Belma as she focused on loving and obeying God and allowed some of her needs to be met through faith-filled, faithful friends, like Lorne Shepherd. We encourage you to get the support of friends and to use the study guide in a discussion group to gain insights from others.

Whether you choose to use one or both of these studies, be blessed with health, hope and understanding. The promise of Jeremiah 29:11–13 is for you: "I know the plans I have for you...to prosper you and not to harm you...to give you hope and a future...You will seek me and find me when you seek me with all your heart" (NIV).

On behalf of Belma and Lorne,
Becky Thomas

P.S. If you haven't yet yielded your life to the Great Physician and Counsellor, why not do it now? Use this prayer as a guide:

Heavenly Father, thank You for loving me today. I know I have erred many times. Please forgive me for these wrongs, and heal me and those I have wronged from sin's effects, even as You heal me from effects of wrongs committed against me. Thank You for providing Your Son, Jesus, who paid for all sin by taking the punishment on His own body through death on a cross. My Healer and Counsellor, I invite You into my heart and choose to live life on Your terms. Amen.

Chapter 1

Terror in the Night

He will cover you with his feathers,
and under his wings you will find refuge...
You will not fear the terror of night,
nor the arrow that flies by day.

PSALM 91:4–5, NIV

It was hot and sticky in Berlin one August night. I was five and a half years old. My grandmother, restless in her sleep beside me, pushed the blanket aside. We shared the only bed in the back of the electrical store and needed no covers on our sweaty bodies. I couldn't sleep, wondering what she had meant when she said, "Something big is going to happen." It didn't sound good.

Oma always seemed to know things before everybody else did. Many times I'd heard the story of Oma's premonition years earlier that something "very bad" was coming. She had stockpiled canned goods and preserved vegetables and fruit from her garden. She had been right. Her preparations helped Oma, Opa and my mom survive World War II while many people died of starvation. For about six months now she had been having similar feelings. When Oma sensed something was about to happen, Opa paid attention.

I could hear Opa snoring beside her. He had come home to our little store late after making house calls to fix electrical problems. He seemed concerned about the intensity of political unrest in Berlin at that time and often talked to Oma about it.

I drank in my beloved grandparents' conversations and, in spite of my age, was aware of the politics in our city.

Since the war the Russians ruled the city's east side and the Allied nations ruled the west. Opa said everyone was talking about the Russians being "very angry" that many people from the east were coming into West Berlin looking for better jobs. The Russians were losing good workers.

Just this week 12,500 had come across. That was 2,000 more than last week.

Oma huffed that it was "their own fault! Who would ever want to stay in East Germany under Communism anyway?" After all, the unfortunate East Berliners were fed up. There were no jobs, and there was no food for them in the Russian-controlled east. I had heard her say she and Opa were relieved that when the city was divided, both our apartment and store were in the west and we didn't have to live under Communism. Now rumours were that the Russians would tighten up the borders so people couldn't get out.

We didn't know that Nikita Khrushchev, the Russian prime minister, had told East Germany they needed to close the border because the mass exodus of citizens was wreaking havoc on the economy. It was all a big secret—until that night!

It was two o'clock in the morning. Unable to sleep, I was lying staring into the darkness when a sudden roar broke the stillness of the night and intensified rapidly.

ATTACKED

Before I could react or process what it might be, the darkness was split by great strobes of light flashing through the store's windows next to the room where we were sleeping.

Oma and Opa were suddenly awake. "Stay! We don't know what's happening," Oma urged me as they jumped out of bed and ran to the front of the store to look outside.

Our little black-and-white wirehaired fox terrier, Purzel, was barking hysterically. Frightened, I stood on our bed crying, trying to see out a window. The street was lit up as if in daytime.

Beams from hovering helicopters illuminated hundreds of people in pyjamas stampeding in confused terror past our store. Screams came from every direction. Opa opened the store's door and stepped out. "What's happening?" he yelled. People were too terrified to respond. Bursts of staccato machine-gun fire intensified the shrieks and piercing screams as Russian soldiers on horseback pounded the pavement in pursuit, trying to kill or capture the unfortunate ones.

My grandparents reacted quickly. Opa grabbed sheets of plywood to board up our store windows and make it look like no one lived there.

Just as quickly Oma, who during the war had seen soldiers kidnap and abuse little girls, grabbed scissors to cut my hair short. I knew she was protecting me. I didn't object to the haircutting. I hugged my bunny close and stifled a sob. My teeth were chattering. I was trembling all over. She put my hair into a ponytail and cut straight across. I covered my face with both hands and didn't even see it fall to the floor.

Reassuring me that everything would be fine, Oma dressed me in boy's clothing and stuffed me in the laundry hamper.

Because of all the chaos, I am not sure of some of the facts. I had the impression that down the street, great slabs of concrete were being lowered from cranes to form a wall between East and West Berlin. So much yelling! So much terror!

Homes and families were ripped apart that night. If a house happened to be in the way, the concrete was dropped right through the middle, either killing the occupants or separating family members who happened to be in different parts of the house.

Those sleeping in one part of the house were instantly in East Berlin. They were tossed on trucks like sacks of sludge and taken away to be slaves. People in the opposite part of the house were now in West Berlin. If the divided families ever saw each other again, it likely wasn't for 29 years—the lifespan of the famous Berlin Wall that now secured the border separating East from West Berlin.

Minutes after Opa finished boarding up the store and we had hidden ourselves, we heard the Russians at the door. The slamming of their fists could have smashed it, but they were kicking it with heavy boots. I was quivering from panic and must have been whimpering because Oma shushed me from outside the hamper. I was sure they would hear my heart pounding if they got in.

Their voices were cold, harsh and merciless. My grandfather had learned to speak some Russian during the war, and he understood them to say, "It's all boarded up. Nobody lives here." The banging ceased. The leaden footsteps paused and receded. Terror left with them. Relief flooded us, and I felt I could breathe again. We were alone once more.

HIDDEN

We continued to hide. Throughout the night we heard yelling, screaming and gunshots. It was horrible to know people were dying on our street.

Afterwards, for three tense weeks we lived like moles in narrow elbow-to-elbow passageways that my grandparents had dug under the store and used during the war. Wherever they turned a corner, these dark tunnels formed small claustrophobic spaces no bigger than two bathtubs. One of these served as our living quarters. It had a long wooden bench on which Oma and I slept. It hurt me that Opa had only the rough, humid stone floor.

Surrounded by spiders and moist concrete walls, we sucked in lungfuls of stale air that smelled of damp earth and longed for a breeze on our faces. We didn't know if it was day or night. Except for periodic thick, low-pitched booms from above that shook the earth around us, it was like living in a tomb. All the while Opa sat with his ear to the radio to hear what was happening while Oma and I spent the time together making up poems, rhymes and stories and playing games. One day Opa said he thought it might be safe for Oma to walk me to school.

DEATH IN THE STREETS

It seemed we emerged into another world. Nothing was the same. I was unsettled and scared. To avoid being noticed, I hid my face and walked with my head down. When I dared look up, I saw the wall. Our house was only half a kilometre from the river where it stood. It was very high. Barbed wire spiralled along its top. Little guardhouses on stilts stood at intervals beside it, and men with machine guns looked out from them. German shepherd dogs were everywhere. Soldiers on horseback patrolled the streets, and most horrifying, people were hanging from trees—dead! They had been murdered by the Russians and left out in the open as a warning.

On the walk to school that day I saw things a little girl should never see. I don't know if Oma thought we would make it there, because the soldiers circled and taunted us like wolves seeking prey. It was horrifying. When we reached the school, we found it surrounded by barbed wire. To get in, we had to find a way around it.

In the school half the children and teachers were missing. We never saw them again. Some had been from the east, but many of the missing had been from West Berlin. We feared they had been kidnapped by the Russians. That day all the classes were amalgamated. I felt confused and bewildered and was grateful that Oma stayed at school with me.

We were to be under the protection of the United States and the Allied nations, but John Kennedy, the president of the United States, was on holidays, and the other countries weren't in any rush to protect us. After all, we were Germans—the nationality associated with Hitler, who everyone said had started the war. The nations didn't like us. As a result, with no protest from anyone, the Russians had freedom to do what they wanted, and we never knew when they might invade the school to beat us up, attack us or violate and haul away our teachers. They kidnapped people to rebuild their decimated labour force and make up for those who had fled from East to West Berlin. Many disappeared.

After that I always felt anxious to have to go to school. For safety and lack of teaching staff, school hours were only from 8 a.m. to 11:20 a.m. It wasn't long before Oma stopped taking me and taught me at home.

One thing remained constant with my schooling. Whether I studied at home or at school, I always enjoyed Oma's loving care. She was there for me. She sat with me every day and helped me with homework. She had an open heart, and I felt safe with her. I could talk to her about everything. To Oma I was *"mein kleines Schätzchen"* (my little precious one). She esteemed me, and it made me feel like a valued human being.

WAR ZONE

I felt safe in our little home, but outside on the street Berlin was a war zone. We weren't allowed to talk about the terrible things that happened. Everything had to be a secret because we didn't know whom we could trust. I remember hearing of a time when Russian soldiers burst into the home of a family we knew and forced the children to watch as they shot and killed their father. They left him bleeding and dead. The family, horror-stricken and grieving, had to dispose of their loved one's body.

On another occasion, I inadvertently got myself in trouble. There was a peephole in the plywood that boarded up our store window. I liked to look through it to see what was happening outside. My grandparents told me repeatedly not to go near it, and I learned a very hard lesson.

One day I snuck into the front part of the store and peered out when Oma wasn't watching. At that moment, a monstrous thing happened. The apartment building across the street disintegrated in all directions with a blast that deafened my eardrums. Bodies flew and fell amidst screams of the injured and dying.

I was undone, frantic, hysterical! The Russians had planted a bomb in the apartment building where my little girlfriend lived. My mind screamed in horror, *What happened to my friend? Is she hurt?*

I ran into the kitchen howling and wailing, and when my grandparents, frightened themselves by the sound of the explosion, realized what I had done, they were very upset. In fact, it was the only time I got a spanking. I promised I would never disobey again, and I meant it. I was so ashamed.

That day affected me deeply. I never saw my friend again.

In retrospect, I don't think it was coincidence that at this very young age I happened to be in Berlin to see the atrocities that took place as the wall went up. God was shaping and mapping my life long before I was five years old. Had I not been there, I doubt I would be here to share my story. Let me start from the beginning.

Chapter 2

Beginnings

If the LORD had not been my help,
my soul would soon have lived in the land of silence.

PSALM 94:17, ESV

I hadn't always lived with my grandparents in Germany. Their daughter Ingeborg, a stunningly beautiful photographer sought by major publications in Europe, had moved to Canada in the early 1950s. That's where I was born and lived for the first 26 months of my life.

When I was young, I didn't know much about my mother—only snatches of what I had heard from my grandparents. But when I was older, I found out more about her from my dad. As a result, I have partially come to understand her enigmatic personality and have been able to reconstruct events in her life with some insight. Here is Ingeborg's story the way I see it.

Just like me, Ingeborg enjoyed an idyllic childhood with my grandparents. But also, like many young women who suffered the effects of the war years in Europe, Ingeborg became a troubled soul. I adored my grandparents, and it was hard for me to understand how someone raised in their home could be so different from them. I experienced the warmth, stability and love of their home for six and a half years, and I knew what her childhood had been like. It was wonderful.

Oma would have prayed to Jesus with her daughter every night just like she did with me. Ingeborg would have known the serenity of playing in the garden with her dolls while her parents pulled weeds and grew delicious fresh fruit and veggies. She would have smelled the aromas of my Oma's kitchen and known the security of sitting at their table. It was a post-Victorian environment—very proper and exceedingly happy. Unfortunately, she wasn't raised entirely in their home.

EFFECTS OF WAR

Fearing for her safety in Germany's political climate of the early 40s, my grandparents had sent 11-year-old Ingeborg to northern Germany to live with friends of her great-aunt. Their desire was to protect her from the harm that could come to young girls during the war. Their efforts backfired.

Before they sent Ingeborg away, she was a sweet, kind, lovely, talkative little girl who enjoyed life with parents who loved her very much. Oma and Opa used to say she was like me when I was with them. But something devastating must have happened to her in the eight years she was away. The war destroyed her.

At 18 Ingeborg returned transformed: sullen, angry, withdrawn, depressed, lacking trust, and quick to lie. She had shut down emotionally and found it difficult to love and be happy. It's anyone's guess what might have happened. She refused to speak of it and was never healed from the psychological and emotional wounds she had experienced. Oma lost her daughter, and it broke her heart.

What happened?

As I now reflect on the circumstances, it seems she had become hardened to life like one who has experienced deep trauma or abuse. Perhaps she tried to protect herself from men or soldiers through lies. I can only imagine. Even if she hadn't been abused, she would likely have felt abandoned, rejected and unloved by her parents. She was young and wouldn't have understood their motives for sending her away.

DISILLUSIONED

When she was 22 years of age the pain of her past had receded just enough to allow Ingeborg to fall in love and become engaged, but the relationship dissolved three years later, and she was devastated. It was more than she could bear.

In an effort to escape the memories, she left Germany and immigrated to Canada, only to discover that pain can't be healed by distance. Heartbreak and trauma kept her bound in chains of suffering. Her effort to distance herself from them was futile, but in her attempt to escape she turned her back not only on painful things but also on the good things of her past—the solid foundation her parents had laid and the abilities that had brought her success in her photography career. She tried to restart her life on empty.

THE ICE PRINCESS

Ingeborg settled in Toronto. Occasionally on weekends she accompanied friends to a dance hall where she sat at a table, her long legs crossed, smoke curling from her lips around her shoulder-length dark hair. Detached, reserved and frozen, she surveyed the activity in the smoke-hazed room but refused to join in.

One of those nights Ingeborg deliberately ignored a handsome young man laughing at a nearby table with his friends. Dark and confident, he attempted to catch her eye with a friendly grin. Twice she noticed him looking at her, but she averted her glance quickly to signal disinterest. One of his friends pointed toward her and said, "Her? Everybody asks her to dance, but she always turns them down."

He was undaunted. Without taking his eyes off her, he pushed away from the table. "She'll dance with me," he said with a smile. He stopped before her, extended his hand and waited. Ingeborg stared into his friendly eyes, put her hand in his and rose to dance. At five feet seven, she was slender and graceful. Bari Basar (Ejubowic)—then known as Gino Ejubowic—moved her masterfully onto the dance floor, where his skills as a ballroom dance instructor showcased the beauty of the mysterious ice princess.

Bari Basar was raised in Yugoslavia, where his father had been a lawyer—the wealthiest man in the country. He had owned restaurants, hotels and many blocks of buildings. In 1945, however, when King Petar surrendered to Tito and the Communist People's Republic of Yugoslavia was established, Bari's father was targeted because of his wealth and education and thrown in jail. His properties were confiscated by the state and his businesses were allocated as state-owned enterprises.

Young Bari was next to be arrested, but to facilitate his escape, he changed his name to *Ejubowic* and fled north to Austria. He was assigned to Refugee Camp Number Five in Klappenberg, where he learned German and lived from 1945 to 1948. When camp residents discovered his talents, they begged him to teach them to dance the Viennese waltz, the English waltz, the foxtrot—all the fashionable dances of the day.

In the meantime, Bari's mother fled with his two sisters to Turkey. Once Bari's dad was released from jail, he left Yugoslavia and moved to Turkey as well. It would be 19 years before Bari would be reunited with his family.

In 1948, when Bari could return to Germany, he chose Salzburg in hopes of finding a job. He had saved some money, and in 1950 he attended Nurnberg University to study electrical engineering—an undertaking he interrupted for a trip to Canada. He hoped to work in Canada for a short time, make some money to send home to his family, learn English and return to Germany to resume life there.

Bari's plans failed. He became entangled with Ingeborg.

TRAPPED

It was 1954. Bari and Ingeborg spent time together, and he noticed her instability. A nurturing, helpful and compassionate man, he wanted to help her develop a stronger sense of herself, but her woundedness ran deeper than he realized, and his attempt to "fix" her was unsuccessful. In a flash of manipulative insecurity, she vowed that if he wouldn't marry her, she would kill herself.

Bari felt trapped. Unwilling for Ingeborg to face such a fate, he rescued her. "I saved her life," he always said thereafter. They married that year in October. Unfortunately it was not for love. Their relationship was grounded in Ingeborg's manipulation and Bari's pity.

Ingeborg didn't tell her parents she was getting married. Even if they had been in Canada, she likely wouldn't have invited them to the wedding. When Oma and Opa found out their daughter had married without telling them, they were grief-stricken. Oma wept the tears only parents abandoned and rejected by a child they love could understand.

In hopes of rebuilding a relationship, Oma and Opa invited the newlyweds to visit. They knew nothing about their son-in-law and worried how they might communicate with him so were pleasantly surprised when Bari greeted them at the airport speaking German.

Oma and Opa adored their daughter's husband. He was handsome, witty and outgoing. He loved people, and people loved him. While Bari engaged everyone in the room, the ice princess sat in a corner hidden behind a book. She rejected attention and let people know she needed no one.

HOPE DEFERRED

In their quiet moments alone, Oma and Opa talked about how wonderful it would be if Ingeborg and Bari would settle in Germany. They contemplated how they might help make it possible and decided to offer Bari 50,000 German marks to start a business.

The idea produced a distinct change in Ingeborg. She loved it and became excited. Her life in Canada had proved unfruitful and she had no reason to return, but Bari could not be persuaded. He didn't want to be "bought," and he refused the offer. Again, my grandparents' hopes were dashed. They grieved, and so did Ingeborg.

Years later Bari confessed he had regretted his decision to reject my grandparents' offer. He blamed himself for altering the course of their lives for nothing more than foolish, youthful pride. He believed that had he consented to live in Germany, things would have been different. That was certainly Ingeborg's contention. Upon their return to Canada, Ingeborg fell into a deep depression.

Who is to say how things might have turned out had Bari and Ingeborg remained in Germany? Ingeborg's personality, rooted in woundedness, would have had the same effect on her relationships whether in Germany or in Canada. Also, a marriage such as theirs, founded on manipulation, was not destined to last.

Bari wanted to introduce his bride to his family in Turkey. He proposed a two-year trial visit, suggesting that Ingeborg might want to settle there, but she refused. It was her revenge for his decision to leave Germany. "I'll go with you to Russia; I'll go with you to China; but I'll never go to Turkey," she insisted. Instead, she became pregnant with me, and she wasn't happy about it.

Forty years later, in a most unusual way, I learned the truth—she hated me before I was born.

REVELATION

At that point in my adult life I had a close personal relationship with God and was attending a conference at a church in Toronto where God's tangible presence was manifest. It was magnetic, irresistible and therapeutic. As people yielded to God, His Spirit filled them with love and healing.

That's what happened to me one evening. The pastor invited people to come forward for prayer, and I was drawn to respond. As he prayed for me, suddenly the Holy Spirit came over me in such a breathtaking, warm, powerful embrace of pure love that I couldn't remain on my feet. My knees buckled and I sank to the floor. As I lay there I had a peaceful sense of being underwater. Puzzled at first, I tried to assess where I was because I lay curled in a fetal position. It seemed as if I was back in my mother's womb. This may sound strange to some, but let me explain.

When God gives one an unusual experience such as this, it's either a resurrected memory or a vision. God allows it for His purposes so He can reveal something otherwise unknown to the individual. In my case, I experienced what is known as an open vision, through which God retrieved a memory for me of what happened before I was born.

The vision of being in the womb was so real that I was totally oblivious to being on the floor in a meeting. I heard talking, but the voices were those of my mother and father arguing. It was as though I was right there with them. My mother was angry at my father because she was pregnant with me.

Then the scene shifted. I became aware of a sharp object penetrating my safe space and coming toward me. As tiny as I was in the womb, I recognized danger, and terror gripped me. My fear was very real. I had nowhere to escape. I pushed as far away from the object as I could, but it jabbed toward me repeatedly. The jabs came and went, seeking to pierce the thin protective membrane surrounding me. Then in a flash the horror of truth flooded me. My mother was trying to kill me.

IN GOD'S HANDS

At that moment I saw two huge protective hands come together and form a wall around me. When the fingers interlocked between me and the sharp object, the frightful blackness gave way to a soft bathing white light, and I felt safe. I knew they were God's hands. A voice that belonged to the hands said, "Just as I was there for you when you fell off the horse, and just as I was there to protect you in your car accident, so I was there right in the beginning to protect you when your mother tried to abort you."

Then as I lay in my mother's womb in total peace, secure in God's protection, Jesus appeared to me. He lifted me out and laid me in the crook of His arm. There were other babies lined up on His arm with me. He walked us into a room where Father God was sitting in Heaven and presented us to Him. God put His hands over us and kissed us. "These ones need a special blessing because they are unwanted. They have been rejected and will have much rejection."

After we were blessed, Jesus walked us back and returned us into the womb, but He didn't leave. He stayed with me in Ingeborg's womb with God's protective presence wrapped around me.

Until that night I didn't know that my mother had tried to abort me. As the vision faded, I lay on the floor, shocked. I wanted to talk to my dad. As soon as I left the meeting, I phoned him. "Dad," I asked, "did Mom try to abort me?"

He gasped. "Who told you that?"

"God did. He told me a lot of other things too. I'm coming over, and I need you to tell me the whole truth." Later, as we talked, he hung his head and acknowledged, "Yes, your mother tried to abort you. Three times."

I have since seen photos taken during abortions. They show the baby in the womb pushing as far from the intruding object as possible. Also, the video *The Silent Scream* (www.silentscream.org) depicts the abortion of an 11-week-old fetus in terrifying detail through the use of real-time ultrasound. As the abortionist's suction tip invades the womb, the child cringes and rears in an attempt to avoid the instrument. Her mouth is visibly open in a "silent scream." Her heart rate increases dramatically to 200 beats per minute as she senses aggression and moves away in a heartrending attempt to escape the instrument.

I didn't have this insight when I lay on the floor at the meeting, but that is exactly what I experienced in my mother's womb. But for the grace of God...

Thus began my life on earth. I was rejected by my mother, not just before birth but, devastatingly so, afterward as well. Not so with my dad. He could hardly wait for me to arrive.

DADDY'S GIRL

In those days men weren't allowed in the delivery room, but my dad worked a 3:00 p.m. to 10:00 p.m. shift at the Toronto Psychiatric Hospital, right beside the Women's College Hospital. He knew the doctors, and the doctors knew him and gave him permission to be in the delivery room when I was born. He donned a gown and helped me make my entrance into the world. When I arrived, he couldn't contain his delight. He held me, kissed me and doted on me.

"My beautiful one!" he exclaimed to me as I lay on his arm. "You are *ma belle*! I want to call her *Ma Belle*," he announced to Ingeborg. "It means 'my beautiful one' in French."

"And what's *that* going to be in English?" my mother objected. "It'll be *Mabel*. No! I don't want that name."

"Fine," he conceded. "We'll turn *Ma Belle* around and call her *Belma*."

Even back then I adored my daddy. I was his little girl, always excited to meet him when he came home from work. He played with me all evening, took me in his arms and danced around the room. It really irritated Ingeborg. She was disinterested in me, but she didn't want him to play with me. She was jealous of my dad's affection toward me, and it caused constant fighting in our home.

Rather than bringing joy to the marriage, my birth increased tension between them. The competition was fierce, with each wanting me to speak their language. My dad speaks nine languages, one of which is Turkish. When he tried to teach me a word in Turkish, she would interject, "No! The word is..." and she repeated it in German.

A year after I was born, Ingeborg got pregnant again. My dad arrived home one day to find blood everywhere. She had successfully aborted a baby boy—my brother. Dad rushed her to the hospital, where she remained for two weeks. When she was released, he urged her go to Germany, visit her parents, rest and recuperate. "Have a little holiday," he suggested. "Take Belma with you and stay a couple of weeks."

I was 26 months old at the time, and my life was about to take a new direction.

Pause and Reflect

Belma had a vision of being in her mother's womb. Ingeborg felt rejected by her mother when she was sent away to live in northern Germany. Often, those who feel rejected reject others. It can create a painful cycle of rejection.

God says He covers us in the womb: "For you formed my inward parts; you knitted me together in my mother's womb" (Psalm 139:13, ESV). "For he will conceal me...when troubles come; he will hide me in his sanctuary. He will place me out of reach" (Psalm 27:5, NLT).

Have you pushed anybody away in order to avoid the pain of rejection or abandonment?

What are some steps you can take to restore that relationship?

Chapter 3

Rooted in Love

For my father and my mother have forsaken me,
but the LORD will take me in.

PSALM 27:10, ESV

My mom and I arrived in Germany to visit my grandparents in the month of April. Ingeborg, depressed and unhappy, concocted a bizarre tale that she had divorced my father. It was another blow to my grandparents. They loved him and had placed his pictures throughout their house. Not realizing the true source of her depression and emotional instability and believing she was now on her own, they suggested she leave the baby with them until she recovered and put her life in order. The idea must have been more than acceptable to Ingeborg, who didn't want the baby in the first place.

"Where is my daughter?" my dad asked, bewildered, when he met her at the airport.

"I left her in Germany," Ingeborg stated.

Fear and helplessness gripped Bari as his mind processed what Ingeborg was saying. "But I'm her father, and I want her," he stammered.

Ingeborg shrugged and retorted, "She's better off there. Her grandparents love her more than you do."

Bari's dismay turned to anger. "I'm buying you a ticket right now. You are going right back to Germany to get my daughter and bring her back to me."

Dad bought the ticket on the spot. Ingeborg got on a plane that night without having left the Toronto airport, flew back to Germany and then returned to Canada without me.

This time when Bari met her at the airport, she announced, "I want a divorce."

"I want my daughter!" he insisted.

Ingeborg had the advantage. "Over my dead body," she spat. "You will never see your daughter again."

SEPARATED

My father went to the chief of police in Toronto, who contacted the chief of police in Berlin. He discovered that he had no legal right over me while I was in Germany. My mother was a German citizen, and he wasn't. I was in her country. What's more, if he were to go to Germany to get me, he would risk being jailed, not because my grandparents would have him arrested but because my mother had the wicked foresight to make such arrangements.

My parents separated but remained in Toronto. One day Bari was driving in the city and saw my mother just ahead of him. He sped up and cut in front of her so she couldn't get away. In the middle of an intersection he jumped from his car and knelt on the pavement beside her door, begging her to bring me home. Delayed cars honked and tried to get around them. She refused him mercy and repeated, "Over my dead body. You will never see your daughter again."

Eight months later Ingeborg called my dad. "If you want Belma, you can go get her. She's with a woman who has a private adoption agency in Toronto." She gave him her number. He immediately called, and the woman confirmed I was there. Identifying himself as my father, he said he would come right away to pick me up.

He arrived at the address. Ingeborg was there with a woman she introduced as the proprietress. She had divorce papers in her hand and demanded that my father sign them before he could see me. In desperation, he signed them. Ingeborg left, and the woman said, "I'll be right back. I'll go get Belma."

My dad waited. The woman didn't return. She had disappeared out the back door. My father not only discovered the place wasn't an adoption agency but found out I wasn't in Canada. He had fallen prey to one of Ingeborg's schemes. He later learned that she had paid the woman to deceive him.

After this incident my father was unable to cope and had to seek psychiatric help. It would be another 19 years before he would see me.

HEAVEN

On the other side of the ocean, however, I was thriving.

One of my richest memories is of spending time outside the city with Oma and Opa on a garden property they had purchased in 1904. We went there every weekend. Without a car it was a 45-minute walk from the underground train near our home in Berlin.

Our garden weekends could not have been more heavenly. My memories of those days—the contented chatter between my grandparents as they worked, the clean air thick with the scent of flowers, the warm breezes, the security—helped sustain me through the horrendous years to come. It was a beautiful garden filled with love and smiles. I'll never forget walking hand in hand along the pathways with Oma, admiring each unique flower and exploring their centres with my nose to find the sweetest aromas.

I loved to be with Oma. Slim, with dark curly hair, she always wore a skirt or dress. I never saw her in slacks, not even in the garden. She was always a lady.

Opa was fun. A little taller than Oma, he was a jolly man. He loved to laugh at life. He, too, was always dressed respectably, including in the garden, where he grew and looked after every kind and colour of flower and fruit tree.

After the war everyone preserved their own produce. Oma canned everything. She loved to put down my favourite fruits—sour cherries, pears, raspberries, plums.

While my grandparents worked, I played house with my doll, rode my tricycle down the pathways, made roads in my little sandbox, and played with Purzel. She and I were great friends. I dressed her in a wedding dress, and we all laughed, seeing her strut with a veil.

The house in the country was a small one-room painted-board structure with no insulation. It contained a plain bench, a chesterfield and a table. At night we put the table on the bench and made a bed where we all slept together.

My great-grandparents had a little house right beside us on the same property. They also came on weekends from their Berlin apartment. They visited us in the garden and brought me candies. I was raised as if they were my grandparents and my grandparents were my parents. A lovely family! I was a blessed child.

Our lifestyle was simple, but it was more than adequate. It seemed abundant and, in today's materialistic world, even enviable.

Our refrigerator was a hole in the ground. Opa climbed down into it and filled a basket for Oma to pull up with a rope. The bathroom was an outhouse, but it seemed perfectly normal, and no one minded. We didn't have running water, and neither did anyone else. We had a pump with an endless supply of cool, clean water. A coal stove and candles took the place of electric heat and lights. We went to bed when the sun went down and got up when it rose.

A Foundation of Faith

Every night we prayed to Jesus, and sometimes Oma told me stories about Him, even though she never spoke of having a personal relationship with Him. Faith probably came down the family line. I can imagine that her mother prayed with her the way she did with me. Oma certainly raised me on Christian principles of honesty, integrity, respect for elders and other godly values. We also celebrated the accepted Christian holidays. Both Christmas and Easter were special.

At Christmas we went to the Roman Catholic Church to see the nativity scene. We also bought a tree, never bigger than me. Opa measured it and said, "Okay, that's the tree." We took it home, put it on the table and decorated it.

All our food was homemade, except the oranges on the lazy Susan in the middle of the table. This was the only time of year we had them. Every delicious treat was placed on it. We gave it a twirl, and whatever stopped in front of each of us, we ate. We swung that lazy Susan all night—just Opa, Oma and me, and we spent a lot of time together. Family was everything.

At Easter we were in the garden house. Oma got up at five o'clock in the morning and put Easter eggs in the flower buds outside. When the sun rose and warmed the petals, they opened, and there were the eggs! One year Opa dressed up in an Easter bunny suit and hopped past us. I thought about it for a moment. "Oma," I said, "I don't want the Easter bunny. I want Jesus." I told her I thought I had been born in the wrong time period. I so would have liked to be born when Jesus lived on earth. Even then, when I was so little, I longed for Him.

PREPARATION FOR LIFE

My grandparents influenced me in many life matters. Among important things I learned from them was how to handle money wisely. They taught me to take a penny and stretch it to ten—a skill that prepared me for the work I do now.

Like so many, we had very little after the war. I went shopping with Oma every week. We wrote a list and visited four stores. In each store we priced the items and recorded the prices. Then we went back to the store that had the best price. Whatever money was left, we hid under the table between the wash pans and saved it.

At five years of age I learned to save. Oma got me play money and showed me how to count it. I stared into her twinkly green-brown eyes as she taught me, loving every moment with her. She made pretend grocery lists of things for me to buy with the money and a game of seeing how much I could save. I played shopping with my little cash register for hours, lining up make-believe money and dolls and pretending to take them to the store to buy things.

Oma also gave me an allowance of ten cents every week, as long as I was a good girl. She said, "We're going to spend five cents and save five." We went to the store with five cents, and she helped me learn how to spend it. She pointed out how value increased through wise choices: "You can get ten of these candies, or five of these. Make sure you get the most for your money."

There were no better people to teach me life skills than my beloved Oma and Opa. Oma taught me how to set the table—knife here, fork there. She taught me good manners and was always proud of me. When we walked down the street and met someone, I had to curtsy. She instilled a strong sense of goodness in me, saying, "This is wrong, but that is right," and she showed me what to do.

My grandparents loved me and gave me a wonderful sense of security, but somewhere in my heart I knew something was missing. Things weren't quite what they were supposed to be, because I wasn't with my parents.

As much as I wanted a mommy, I especially felt my daddy's absence. I looked at him and my mother in photographs and thought how handsome he was. I could feel that he had adored me, and my heart ached to be with him. I stared at his picture and wished I could see him. I didn't understand why he never came to visit. My mother came only once, when I was four years old, and I remember her pushing my stroller. I was so happy, thinking, *I've got my mommy! I've got my mommy!* I knew this was the way it was supposed to be.

When I was five and a half, Ingeborg sent me a parcel from Canada. Oma always spoke positively of her. "Look!" she said, handing me the package. "Your mommy sent you these sweaters." Out of my mouth came the words, "Why would she send me all these sweaters if she doesn't love me?" My young mind had grasped the truth.

SCHOOL DAYS

Kindergarten was just around the corner from us in a Protestant church run by Catholic nuns. I liked it, but it made me nervous. The nuns who taught there were strong, loud women and made me feel uneasy. It cost money for parents to send children to kindergarten, and for that reason I was only there in the morning. At noon Oma picked me up, because in the afternoon we only had lunch and a nap.

On the day Oma enrolled me in grade one I felt a particular twinge of sadness. I loved my grandparents, but I was almost ashamed that I didn't have parents. Everyone else was with their mom and dad, but I was with my grandmother.

I was afraid I wouldn't do well in school. In some ways I felt stunted or incomplete—unable to move ahead without my mother and father. I was different because my parents didn't want me and I had to be raised by my grandparents.

In grade one we learned to read, write and do math. Then in grades two and three, we learned to print. Math in Germany was about four years ahead of the Canadian curriculum.

Every day when I went home Oma helped me with homework. She always pumped encouragement and delight into her "little precious one." At times she taught me songs she wrote, and we did little dances together.

Another joy I experienced with my grandparents was life at the store they owned. After the war, many people didn't have electricity. Opa, being an electrician, fixed their lamps and restored electricity to homes that were bombed out. Oma got up at three o'clock in the morning and pulled a little wagon to the next town. At the garbage dump she filled it with scrap metal, which Opa used for making lamps. He installed wiring in people's homes and sold them his homemade lamps.

HOME AT THE STORE

My grandparents were really hard workers and made a million dollars in 13 years because ours was one of the busiest stores in town. Opa sold his lamps there, and Oma tended the counter. She was conscious of her appearance. Her hair had turned white when she was 30 years old from the traumas of war. "People don't want to see an old lady behind the counter," she quipped, and she dyed her hair dark.

I spent a lot of time at the back of the store. It was home to me. Oma's kitchen was there, with space for me to play. Some days Oma wore a path from the storefront to the kitchen, where she cooked and baked. The aroma of strudel baking always filled the air. I also recall her making liver and onions once a month. When she made it, it tasted wonderful!

There was a Murphy bed in a room between the storefront and the kitchen. Sometimes we slept there to deter burglars. It wasn't uncommon for Oma to spot thieves and run out the door and down the street after them.

She was often alone in the store, looking after things by herself while Opa worked at someone's house. I felt sorry for her. Even then I wondered how she managed all her tasks and me.

I was mesmerized by Oma's stories about the war. One particular story of running for cover gave her nightmares.

WAR AND DANGER

Before bombers came, she said, two warning sirens sounded. At the first one, people had five minutes to get to the bunker. On one occasion when the siren wailed, she ran to the bunker, but some friends who lived on the same street didn't hear it. They didn't run for cover until the second siren. By that time, they only had three minutes to get to safety. Panicked, they ran to the shelter, but it was too late. The plane carrying the bomb roared overhead. Oma turned to look just as the bomb dropped. Its heat liquefied the asphalt, and the street became a molten river that buckled over the people like a wave, swallowing them and burning them alive. Oma heard their dying screams and watched in horror as they disappeared.

Each time she told this story she relived the grief of losing her friends and being the only one to survive. As a little girl I listened spellbound, hoping my presence would comfort her.

Oma told me story after story, crying and feeling pain for those who had suffered. Whenever Oma could, she tried to alleviate suffering. I remember how many times she reached out to others, especially to one single mom whose son, Rainer, was my best friend.

I never learned what happened to Rainer's father. Perhaps he had died in the war, but I felt very sad for Rainer because he didn't have a daddy. My grandparents used to help his mom however they could—with groceries or electrical needs. Rainer and I played together when his mother came over. I remember her wiping tears as she and Oma talked. Meanwhile Rainer and I made great, long games of hopscotch on the sidewalk with chalk—a luxury—and hoped it wouldn't rain to wash away our drawings.

Even though my life seemed to be near-perfect and the night of the Berlin Wall terror was behind us, danger still prevailed in Berlin. At our country house, my grandparents were always alert, not knowing when a Russian soldier might appear. Fortunately, Oma's premonitions always warned us in time, and Opa never questioned them.

Once while we were in the garden, she sensed that something was wrong and warned Opa to be prepared for "a dangerous intruder" that day. Right away Opa turned the furniture in our little house upside down and sprinkled dirt on it and on the floor. It looked abandoned. Sure enough, four hours later the Russians came.

Opa had built a hiding place under the floor, and we scrambled down into it. Oma held her hand firmly around Purzel's snout. From where we were hiding we could see the boots of the Russians marching toward our house. The soldiers opened the door and looked inside. Opa understood them to say, "Oh, we must have already been here. There is nothing here. It's been dealt with."

No matter how frightening things were, I always felt safe because I lived in my grandparents' love. Had we lost everything or had nowhere to live, it wouldn't have mattered, as long as we were together as family. My life was built on a foundation of love and security that strengthened me to endure the coming years. Regardless of how horrendous things became, my grandparents had given me a plumb line for what was right and healthy and what was wrong and abnormal. Soon that knowledge tested my very life, but God had a plan.

Pause and Reflect

Although Belma had not prayed a specific prayer to ask Jesus to come into her life, she accepted Him at this very young age by indicating a desire to include Jesus in her life. Her desire to choose Jesus over the Easter bunny was a statement of faith in Christ. For her to remember expressing that desire so clearly out of so many conversations she had as a child indicates that it had a profound effect on her that lodged in her mind and spirit.

Have you made a life decision to get to know God?

Have you been introduced to Jesus?

Belma's Oma experienced deep trauma from the war, evidenced by the fact that her hair turned white when she was only 30 years old. Yet we will see that she remained gentle and kind-hearted.

Have you suffered the effects of a traumatic event or time period in your life?

If so, in what ways have those difficult experiences changed you?

Are there areas of your life that you would like Jesus to transform and redeem?

Chapter 4

In the Clutches of a Monster

Even though I walk through the darkest valley,
I will fear no evil, for you are with me;
your rod and your staff,
they comfort me.

PSALM 23:4, NIV

When I was seven and a half, a letter came from my mother. I remember Oma's countenance changing as she read it. Fear filled her eyes; she panted, caught her breath and covered her mouth with her hand. Something terrible had happened! "What's wrong, Oma? What's wrong?" I cried in alarm.

We were standing in the kitchen at the back of the store. Still grasping the letter with trembling fingers, she spoke in measured words, her eyes brimming with tears and lips set to keep them from quivering: "Your mother has just written to say she wants you to go live in Canada." The impact of Oma's words now registered on me, and we looked into each other's eyes in desperation. Our world was about to fall apart.

Oma was heartbroken. Her pain washed over me. I ran to her, buried my face in her apron and burst into tears. How could I leave my beloved Oma? This was my home.

Ingeborg had remarried. She was under pressure from her new husband, Helmut, to retrieve me from my grandparents and have me live with them in Canada. In his opinion, if my mother had a daughter, she should be with her.

In addition to the pressure from Helmut, I now think my mother may not have wanted me to remain bonded with my grandparents and have a wonderful life. She had been jealous of my relationship with my father, and judging from the way she eventually treated me, she was likely jealous of my relationship with Oma and Opa.

A Bad Year

It was 1963—a bad year. President Kennedy was shot, the Profumo scandal rocked European politics, a tsunami killed 22,000 people in Pakistan, the Great Train Robbery shocked England, and my grandparents took me across the ocean to live with my mother in Toronto.

I had to leave everything. When the last day of my life with my family in Germany ended, I said goodbye to my friends, teachers, great-grandparents—everyone in the community. Ingeborg told my grandmother I would have all new things when I got to Canada. At my mother's demand, I was to leave all my belongings. The only things I took were my dolls.

As hard as it was for me, it was devastating for Oma and Opa. Oma had missed my mother's youth during the war, and she was deeply grateful to God for giving her a second chance to enjoy childhood with me, another "daughter."

But those sweet days came to an abrupt end. Oma, Opa and I travelled from Germany to Canada on an ocean liner—a terrible 21-day journey. The worst trip of my life! I was so nervous I could hardly talk. I knew I was going to live with strangers who didn't even want me, let alone love me. The thought of having to leave the love and safety of my grandparents made me physically ill.

We landed in New York harbour on October 26, 1963.

America! Land of the Free

Everything was strange and unfamiliar. I couldn't understand the language. For a little country girl from Germany the strange voices, smells of the city and huge buildings were overpowering. I clutched my container of dolls. The customs officer, who looked like a Russian soldier to me, yanked it out of my hand and flung my dolls mercilessly onto the dock, where they landed with sickening thuds and lay as though dead. I reacted in horror and panic, like any mother would. My dolls! My precious "children"! I screamed in hysteria that my beloved ones were being so mindlessly brutalized. The officer laughed at me. With neither sympathy nor remorse, he took my response as proof we must be hiding things, and he badgered my grandparents with question after question.

He thought we might have hidden something we shouldn't be bringing into the country in the dolls.

BULLIED

In those days the stench of Hitler's regime still clung to every German citizen, and this officer made it clear we weren't welcome. He treated us as if he believed we deserved punishment for Hitler's brutality and wanted us to know he disdained us.

As the interrogation intensified, my grandparents became increasingly flustered, confused and disoriented because they didn't understand English. I saw it as an attack by authority figures that represented danger, and I was terrified.

When things finally calmed down, I was allowed to retrieve my dolls. We gathered our possessions and boarded a train from New York to Toronto.

Exhausted from the ordeal, we settled into our overnight berths relieved to rest, but it wasn't over.

In the middle of the night another set of customs officers strode through the train car, banged on our door and barged into our room. Again they demanded our passports, interrogated my grandparents and searched our belongings. Their authoritarian presence and threatening demeanour filled the room. Despite my tiredness, they demanded I get up and take off my clothes so they could check for contraband.

Again my poor Oma and Opa were at the mercy of bullies because they couldn't understand English. Despite the language barrier, Oma caught enough to realize they were discussing taking me away from them. That was beyond terrifying for all of us.

Oma became a mad woman! She screamed in a way I had never heard before and with an authority no one dared question. After some minutes they backed down, turned and walked away, leaving us trembling. None of us slept after that.

As light dawned the metal wheels screamed to a halt at Union Station in Toronto.

That same day, October 30, unbeknownst to us, my dad flew from Toronto to Turkey to visit his family. There he met Ayla, his current wife, and remarried. At the same time, he changed his last name, *Ejubowic*, back to the Yugoslavian *Basar*. After their six-month honeymoon he and Ayla settled in Toronto. How ironic that I arrived under his shadow! We had been that close!

THE HEART OF DARKNESS

As we disembarked, Oma caught sight of my mother. "Look," she said bending toward me, "there's your mother. Go hug her. That's the proper thing to do."

My first thought was, *That's my mother! She's just like her pictures!*

I hesitated at the sight of the strange woman. I saw the man standing beside her and didn't want to leave the safety of Oma's loving embrace. Oma gave me a little push. I wanted to please her, so I ran toward this living photograph and threw my arms around her, exclaiming, "Mommy, Mommy!"

It was like embracing a steel statue. Instead of hugging me back, she pushed me away. Her eyes met mine for a millisecond—black, piercing, empty. My head and heart froze. Everything seemed to stop. It was the first time I experienced rejection, and it felt like I had been slapped in the face.

I glanced furtively at the man beside my mother, my new stepfather, Helmut. His face registered no emotion. No connection. Empty.

I didn't want Oma to know I was distressed, so I said nothing. Strangely, as close as I was to my grandparents, in my mother's presence an impenetrable invisible curtain fell between them and me. It stole freedom and intimacy from our relationship and locked me in a prison of solitary confinement. Suddenly I was unable to share my heart with them.

No one spoke during the drive from Union Station to my mother's house. I was still in shock from the cold rejection, and I'm sure my grandparents must have been dying inside. Their precious granddaughter was trapped in circumstances no one could change.

When we walked through the front door of my mother's three-storey townhouse, I saw walls without warmth. *This isn't a home,* I thought. *It's just a house!* The interior was stark and harsh—foreign to me and bland, as if it were abandoned. I shivered.

They introduced me to Helmut's teenage daughter, who was totally disinterested, and then showed me my room. Walls. A thin cot for a bed.

One dresser. That was it. Cold and desolate! Panic rose in me, but words wouldn't come.

Later I learned that Helmut's first wife had died shortly before he met my mother. His 14-year-old daughter had to live with her dad. My mother had been charming to the poor girl before the wedding, but when the honeymoon was over, she became the wicked stepmother who made the girl's life as miserable as possible. To have a little sister who couldn't speak English thrown into the mix was too much for her, so she ignored me.

Like Cinderella, I slept in the cold, stark room that night, fearful of what was to come.

The next day was Halloween. We didn't have Halloween in Germany, and I had no idea what it was. Ingeborg took an old bedsheet, cut two holes in it for eyes, tossed it over my head, gave me a bag and said, "There. Go knock on doors. They'll give you candy."

I was afraid, but I didn't dare protest. Thankfully Helmut's daughter went with me, but her unfriendly presence added to my discomfort. Looking back, I don't know how I managed to last through the ordeal. I felt alone and disoriented, anxious and depressed. To not understand the language and go door to door under a white bedsheet with a surly, distant girl was a nightmare.

SHREDDED

During the three weeks my grandparents were there, Ingeborg did everything she could to keep us separated. It was heartrending for me and for them. We had planned that I would go with them to the airport when they left, but that day, as I came down the stairs ready to go, my mother held out her hand and said, "Halt! You're not going. You're staying here." My grandparents were already out the door, so I couldn't even say goodbye.

Apparently they asked where I was. When they realized what my mother had done, they rushed back in to look for me. Still in shock and sobbing at the top of the stairs, I ran down into Opa's arms. He was beside himself, bewildered, frantic—hardly able to breathe. Oma choked back tears and couldn't speak. Her look betrayed her understanding that they had released me into the clutches of a monster. At that moment we were ripped apart in flesh and spirit. Our family unit was rent.

I thought many times about my grandparents on their three-week journey back to Germany with a huge void in their hearts where a kiss should have been. Later I found out that Oma cried the whole trip. When she got home, she sent me a letter, but I didn't receive it. Except for the odd one right at the beginning, my mother intercepted all my grandparents' letters. I assume she cut off communication between us because she couldn't tolerate the intimacy we shared. Jealousy had hardened her heart.

MISFIT

I can't remember much about the first days in my new school, and I would be happy to forget them altogether. The German education system was far more advanced than the Canadian one, but I couldn't excel in my schoolwork because I couldn't speak English.

Kids laughed at my strange clothes and inability to speak their language. The teacher was even less understanding. She made me read out loud in class. I tried to read phonetically but pronounced everything the German way. For instance, *the* I pronounced *tay*. There is no "th" sound in German.

I had to protect myself at recess. The kids chased me around the schoolyard shouting, "Hitler! Hitler! She's Hitler!" When they caught me, they hit me.

At lunchtime, I was horrified at the waste. If kids didn't like the food in their lunch boxes or didn't want to eat it, they threw it away. I couldn't understand how anyone could throw away good food.

My one bright spot at school was an overweight girl by the name of Izzy Turner. No one included her in activities, but she was very kind to me. My self-appointed bodyguard, she was my place of refuge because she protected me. No one dared challenge her.

INCIDENTS WITH INGEBORG

The next seven years with my mother were a nightmare of abuse. I desperately wanted to talk to my dear grandparents, but they were out of reach. Had I not experienced a normal, stable environment of love with them, I don't think I would have survived. Throughout all those years I held on to the good times—happy memories that breathed hope in me for my tomorrows. I learned that if you know that someone loves you, you can get through the toughest times.

Many times I longed for Oma's love to lift me out of pain and suffering. One day I fell outside and scraped my knee badly. I could see pebbles in it, and it hurt. I ran into the kitchen and showed my mother. She glanced at it, turned the other way and said nothing. She was angry that I had bothered her. I was on my own. What to do? I tried to think what Oma might have done and used a facecloth to clean my knee as best I could.

Painful incidents with Ingeborg are still vivid in my mind. Happier days came eventually, and so did complete release from every hurtful memory. I can describe these incidents now without emotional pain. I am sad to say that many who have suffered the way I did do not recover, but there is a way. Let me share some episodes with Ingeborg first.

Ingeborg really was like a wicked stepmother. She had written to Oma saying she would provide me with everything new when I came to Canada, but that didn't happen. Only once did she buy me something new—a pair of ugly shoes several sizes too big. Whatever belonged to me, she took away. She even took away my dolls.

I arrived in Canada wearing a little pale-blue cotton dress Oma had bought me, and that's what I wore every day for four years. As I grew, the dress got shorter and shorter. It was very embarrassing. Oma had taught me modesty and instilled in me a consciousness to cover my body properly. When the dress became way too short, every day on my way to school I hid in an alley behind some garbage cans, took it off, and made it into a skirt. It helped cover my bare legs. With my sweater buttoned overtop, it looked like a long skirt. On the way home I went back into the alley and changed it back into a short little dress in a vain attempt to allay my mother's beatings.

I didn't really care that I didn't have nice clothes. For some reason, the kids didn't seem to notice that I wore the same thing all the time. Occasionally one asked, "Why are you wearing that again?" and I'd say, "That's all I have."

All I cared about was to be covered up. I wanted something that would fit and keep me warm. I had a hat, mitts, boots and a sweater-coat from Germany. It too was soon too short, and my legs were exposed in sub-zero weather. I was very cold walking to school, especially at -20°

Celsius. When I was about 12, Ingeborg gave me back some dresses I had brought from Germany, and I used them to make a skirt.

I often wondered at Ingeborg's beautiful clothes. Her nails were perfectly manicured, and she looked impeccable. She spent a lot of time and money beautifying herself. She not only neglected me, but she purposely harmed me.

Ingeborg worked as a cashier at a grocery store, and when she went to work, she left me lists of things to do. One day she wanted me to do the dusting. I was still dusting when she came home, but she looked around and said, "You didn't dust."

I said, "I dusted."

"You are lying! You *did not dust!*"

My heart sped up. I felt frightened and vulnerable. "I'm not lying! I really *did* dust."

She lunged at me. "*You are lying!*" she screamed. A hard slap landed on my face. I raised my arms and ducked, but she pummelled me like a punching bag. Her hands grabbed me. I jerked like a ragdoll as she heaved me against the wall. She kept slapping, pushing, even kicking me and screaming all the while that I had lied and hadn't done what she told me to do. I lay curled against the wall, crying, wailing, begging for mercy, with my arms wrapped around my head for meagre protection. Suddenly a huge blow landed across my back and sent crushing pain through me. I could hardly breathe. I realized she had grabbed the broom and was bringing it down with all her force on me, again and again, until the handle snapped.

Then it stopped. There was a change in her voice. "Okay," she purred as though she was satisfied, as though she had acquired something she wanted. Then she stated flatly, "You're grounded, and that's it."

I was grounded for a month. That meant I wasn't allowed proper food and wasn't permitted to play outside. I had to remain locked in my room.

This grounding was the first of many. Most of my life with Ingeborg I was grounded, because, according to her, I was always "bad." Through my window I watched life go by outdoors as my friends played. I was allowed to go to school, but when I was grounded, she called my teachers and told them to keep me inside and not allow me out to play. She thought ahead how to make things worse for me.

Another time she came in my room and told me I had to strip the floors of wax and put on new wax. I did it the only way available. I scraped it all off by hand, and it was hard work. I smoothed it off and got all the wax out of the corners. Then I washed the floor, put on new wax, and polished it to a bright shine. It took me about four hours. She came in to inspect my work, and anger reared in her. "Not good enough. Take it off and do it again!" Her words, steeped in hatred, sliced through the air like knives. I did it again. Another four hours.

In grade five, they gave us each a little gold Gideon Bible at school. I was very excited because I was familiar with the Bible. In Germany religion had been one of our school subjects. We studied the life of Jesus and wrote little stories on Bible topics as early as grade one. What a treasure it was to have my own Bible! I was delighted. I wanted to write my name in it.

I knew my dad's surname to be *Ejubowic*. In Germany I had used my grandparents' last name, and in Canada Ingeborg had given me her current husband's last name. Since this was my own Bible, I decided to write my "real" name in it. On the first page, I wrote, "Belma Diana Ejubowic."

I went home excited. I showed the Bible to my mother. She opened it and uttered a scream at the top of her lungs. "Don't you *ever* let me see you *ever* write that name again! *Ever!*" Before I could recoil she grabbed my arm, picked me up, threw me against the wall and hit me on my head over and over again.

THE BEATINGS

The beatings came almost daily. There were times I was so black and blue I couldn't go to school. My dress wouldn't cover my bruises. My mother regularly broke broom handles over me. She beat me so hard, my body was black.

Once while she was pounding me, I remember thinking, *I'm totally flat!* I felt crushed, like a bowl of nuts ground with a pestle! There was nothing left of me. Every day she beat me on top of the bruises from the day before.

At first I tried to resist the beatings, but they always happened so fast, I couldn't get away. The pain was horrific. The punches, kicks and blows sent shooting pains throughout my body. I screamed in agony every time. She taunted me, "If you move, it'll be worse. Stay still. If you keep moving away from me, I'll keep beating you." I had to stay put.

Another time she took me out to a country place she and Helmut owned. Inside their frame house she beat me terribly, throwing me against the walls. I remember every moment. I was trapped! Terrified, I thought, *When am I going to get out of this?* I always had hope I would make it. When she finished, she walked away. I had nothing left in me. I lay shaking and exhausted, unable to cry. Did she want me dead?

At times the pain choked me. People usually dissociate during such abject trauma and develop alternate personalities that hide their pains, but that didn't happen to me. My healing would have been more difficult had I developed multiple personalities through dissociation. But I was always there, feeling everything.

I constantly tried to cover up my bruises. In my mind the beatings were embarrassing and shameful. I tried to keep them a secret because I felt the shame would somehow reflect on me.

My mother forever berated me. "You're a mistake," she snarled. "You should never have been born. You're just like your father. He was a liar, and you're a liar." She tried to destroy any sense of value in me.

LIVING A NIGHTMARE

I remembered how Oma prayed to Jesus, and I would ask Him to help me. I look back now and realize that Jesus was there. But another entity was there as well. A spiritual enemy was trying to destroy me through my mother.

My stepsister lived with us only briefly. When she was 15 she moved in with an older woman in our city because she couldn't tolerate my mother's abuse. My mother didn't beat her the way she beat me, but she didn't feed her. The girl quit school and took a job to support herself. Occasionally she came to the house and snuck in some food for me. I really appreciated it. Because of Ingeborg's jealousy, Helmut met his daughter in secret without my mother knowing.

Ingeborg's jealousy affected all of us. I was neither allowed a relationship with Helmut nor permitted to be in his presence without her. She forbade him to talk to me and parent me, because I was her daughter and under her control. While she was at work, I was to remain in my room.

She and Helmut fought constantly, but she had the final word. Their relationship reminds me of the biblical King Ahab and his wife, Jezebel. It was the same with Ingeborg and Helmut. She was in control, and he was forced to obey her.

Once, when I was 11, Helmut was three doors down the street, talking with a neighbour, while my mother was beating me in our basement. Helmut came home and said, "Stop it, Ingeborg. The neighbours can hear her screaming." My mother was livid. She threw me in the car, drove me out to the country and dragged me into the woods, where she could beat me without anyone hearing.

Another day my mother was putting on a nice luncheon for friends. She made a plate for me with about five bites on it. Someone commented, "She has to eat more than that!" Ingeborg invented a blatant lie: "She doesn't know when to stop. She overeats and makes herself very sick, so I have to control what she eats." They believed her.

I wasn't allowed good food, and neither was I allowed to eat at the table with Ingeborg and Helmut. I ate by myself at the kitchen counter on a stool. My mother left me mouldy food on a plate—jam on toast—and often put my milk out the night before so that by the time I drank it, it was sour and had scum on top. If I didn't eat, she beat me. When she beat me her eyes turned a fiery dark red and I could see evil inside.

As long as I lived at Ingeborg's, I slept on the sagging army cot, and I was not allowed to wash in the bathroom. I had to use the basement laundry tub. One day while I was standing on the cold cement floor I thought, *Why am I down here? I shouldn't be here. I'm a human being!* It dawned on me that my mother was being inhumane to me the way some people said Hitler had been to the Jews. I compared my experience with theirs, and it seemed as if she was functioning under the same spirit. She had lived through the war and had not only seen how the Jews were treated but likely been subjected to similar cruelty. Cruelty was woven into the fabric of who she was. Her frightening rage could erupt at the smallest provocation.

REUNION

The day I had longed to see finally arrived when I was 12. My grandparents came to visit. My hopes were soon crushed. Ingeborg made sure I wouldn't have time to be with them. She wrote me a huge list of chores with crazy things on it, like going into the forest to gather wood—anything to keep me apart from my grandparents. If I didn't complete the list, I would be grounded and wouldn't be able to see them at all.

During the brief times I saw them, I tried to convey how badly my mother treated me, but they were bewildered. "How can that be?" they asked. I explained I wasn't getting their letters, but they found that hard to believe as well. Three weeks later they went back to Germany, and I had hardly seen them.

FED UP

I treasured the few letters from my grandparents that Ingeborg had allowed me to have and read them many times. One day when I was 13 she came into my room and was about to take them, but that broke me. I flew into a rage that rivalled any eruption of hers and screamed that I would kill her. I lunged at her, livid with anger, wielding only a book, but I felt like I was drawing from a reservoir of massive supernatural strength. She knew I was serious, and she turned and ran. She never did take the letters.

In my years with Ingeborg, that was the only time I exploded. I may have been particularly sensitive because she had just threatened me with a hot iron, and the incident was fresh on my mind.

DEAD ENDS

I knew my mother's behaviour wasn't normal. She had her own issues. I wasn't mistreated for anything I had done. The relational foundation and healthy understanding my grandparents instilled in me gave me strength to know who I was and that I didn't deserve such abusive treatment.

Another hope that helped me survive was the knowledge that I had a dad who loved me. It fanned an anticipation that I could escape my nightmarish existence. I wanted to find my dad. The last I had heard, he lived in Toronto, but I had no idea where.

When life became completely unbearable, I took matters into my own hands. During the summer when I was 14, I snuck out of the house with my dad's picture in my pocket while my mother was at work and hitchhiked from the town we were living in to Toronto to look for him. Truck drivers picked me up. I'm amazed I wasn't afraid to do it. Now I think I must have had an angel assigned to me, because I was protected.

I had no idea where to search. Wherever the driver dropped me off, I went door to door showing the picture and asking, "Do you know this man? He's my father, and I am looking for him." I didn't know my efforts were futile because my dad had changed his name.

I would be gone all day, hitchhike back, and make it home before my mother and Helmut arrived from work. Somehow my mother became suspicious. The last four weeks of summer, before she left for work, she locked me in my room with no food or water. It was endless torture. The hours and days crawled by as I sat at my window and watched people outside. But after a few weeks of isolation, I got an idea.

I climbed out the window onto the roof. From there, I jumped to the ground and got back on the road to resume dad-hunting. When I arrived home I climbed a ladder to my window and hoped Ingeborg wouldn't see it before I could put it away.

My search yielded no results, and I had to reconsider my approach. It occurred to me that at the airport I would have access to Toronto's phone books. If I looked up his name, I reasoned, I could find him.

I hitchhiked to the terminal and found one Ejubowic. When I called the number, a man answered. "I'm looking for my dad, Bari Ejubowic," I told him. "My name is Belma. Is my dad there?" He said no but told me he was my brother. He was playing games with me, and it really upset me. I asked again, "But where is my dad?" Finally he told me my dad didn't live there.

I was exasperated. I didn't know what more to do. Years later, when I talked to my dad, he said he knew that man. People had always confused them. "If only he had called me," he lamented, "I would have known you were looking for me." It would be another seven years before I found him.

It's a gross understatement to say that living with my mother was depressing. The question of how to escape was foremost in my mind, and I called on God to help me. After one beating, while I was locked in my room I had an open vision of a very long tunnel. At the end was a light. I knew if I held Jesus' hand and kept walking step by step through the darkness, one day I would reach the light. From then on, the vision strengthened me and kept me going. One day I would move out of my mother's house.

That day was coming. I was 14 and happened to be at my neighbour's. I had written letters to my grandparents. I asked if she could mail them and receive my grandparents' letter in return. The opportunity came to tell her about the abuse I was suffering. I could finally communicate with someone, but both my grandparents and neighbours were very concerned what might happen if Ingeborg found out.

Another barrier! I felt helpless at the lack of options.

About that time Ingeborg again flew into a rage at me. I was running up the stairs away from her when in her fury she grabbed one of the metal rods that held the stair runner in place and threw it at me. Fortunately the rod didn't hit me, but it flew past me right through the window. The neighbours were sitting in their yard, and it landed next to their baby. They called the police. My mother, deviously clever, put a "no trespassing" sign on the lawn and threatened to sue them if they came onto our property. She managed to keep them away.

The incidents seemed to be getting increasingly bizarre, and my ability to endure them was diminishing. One of the last was the hair episode.

HUMILIATED

I owned one precious thing—my long wavy hair down to my waist. My identity was wrapped up in it. I felt beautiful in my hair, and I loved it. The day before I was to start high school, my mother decided to cut it off. I begged her, "Not my hair! Please don't cut it!" She seemed to have joy— like a perverse delight or excitement—about cutting it. I can't tell you how humiliating it was to hear the scissors grinding through my thick mane. Gone! All my lovely hair! Chopped off! My stepsister was visiting and witnessed the ordeal but couldn't intervene.

The only other preparation Ingeborg made for my high school debut was to purchase new shoes for me. Ignoring the fact that my feet were size 6, she bought ugly size 11 oxfords. They were the only shoes I had. I either went barefoot or wore them.

One day, just before starting classes, a friend told me about the Children's Aid. They said it was a place that helped children. I asked if her mom could take me there, and she agreed. Hesitant at first but increasingly bold, I showed them my bruises. The workers were disgusted and very sympathetic. They went to my mom's house unannounced so she would not have time to put up the "no trespassing" sign.

Children's Aid couldn't do much in those days. The workers talked to my mother, but they were afraid of her. From that time on, until we moved, my mother didn't lay hands on me.

After the Children's Aid episode we moved again, and the beatings resumed. This time my mother and Helmut were building a new house. When the basement was dug, huge loads of heavy concrete blocks were delivered for the foundation walls. My mother told the contractor and his workmen that I would carry the blocks to them. They stood around and waited as I carried each block, one by one, for them to place.

Ingeborg and Helmut moved often. One year I attended three different high schools. Regardless of where we moved, she found a way to humiliate me. At one school, I had to take summer classes. In the heat of July my mother made me wear a coat, hat and mitts. Of course the kids laughed. Teachers must have wondered what kind of woman would send a child to school dressed like that.

At another school my class was learning a special Polish dance. We planned to perform it for our parents and were very excited. Perhaps I have been endowed with some of my father's natural gifting because I loved to dance. I practiced and worked hard at learning my part. I could hardly wait to perform it. The night of the performance I got ready, but my mother wouldn't let me go. With one dancer missing, the performance failed. The next day, no one talked to me. They assumed I had simply not bothered to show up.

DONNA

While in high school, I made friends with a girl named Donna. One day she stopped me in the hallway and asked, "Belma, is everything all right at your house? My mother called your mom last night to see if you could come for the weekend, but your mom hung up. We called back, and there was no answer. Is anything wrong?"

I stepped back nervously, not knowing what to say. No one was supposed to know my problems, but Donna persisted. She continued prodding, and I spilled the whole story. Shocked and sympathetic, she went home and told her parents. They took me out of school and after they heard my story called the police and Children's Aid.

I told them that Children's Aid came to our previous house and I only had a short reprieve from the beatings. They asked if my grandparents might take me back, but I didn't think that was possible. I was out of ideas. I almost gave up, thinking there was no point in anyone trying to help me. As it turned out, God had a plan.

Pause and Reflect

When someone is jealous it doesn't mean that they love you; it means they want to own you. "For jealousy makes a man furious, and he will not spare when he takes revenge" (Proverbs 6:34, ESV). "Who can stand before jealousy?" (Proverbs 27:4, ESV). "Love is strong as death, jealousy is fierce as the grave. Its flashes are flashes of fire, the very flame of the LORD" (Song of Solomon 8:6, ESV). Belma's mother suffered from an extreme and abnormal jealousy toward her daughter, causing her to act abusively.

What do you believe was the cause of such jealousy?

Jealousy can be described as a green-eyed monster. Have you ever had to wrestle with the green-eyed monster?

Whether it was your own jealousy or someone else's, describe how you reacted and felt when confronted with it.

We are a peculiar people. So often we feel great shame or pain, and we don't want others to know it. Why? Because we think others might reject us if they knew who we really are. We think we have to present an "acceptable" version of ourselves to others. We "cover up" and try to look good on the outside while on the inside we are a huge mess.

But what is inside manages to come out whether we like it or not. That seemed to be the case with Ingeborg. It seemed she wanted to look perfect on the outside to compensate for and cover up her intense inner pain and imperfections.

Think of a time when you could no longer hold back your thoughts and they exploded out of you.

What spilled out? Was it praise, anger, frustration?

If it was negative, how could you have aired your laundry in a healthier way?

Satan was trying to destroy Belma, to short-circuit God's plan for her life through the harm and abuse inflicted by Belma's mother. The enemy knows that God has a plan for our lives, and his goal is to thwart it. Jesus depicts the enemy as a thief: "The thief comes only to steal and kill and destroy. I came that they may have life and have it abundantly" (John 10:10, ESV).

Can you identify a moment when you felt emotionally stuck in time, unable to get past the pain of a memory?

How does this memory play out in your life today?

Chapter 5

Escape from Hell

"For I know the plans I have for you," declares the LORD,
"plans to prosper you and not to harm you,
plans to give you hope and a future."

JEREMIAH 29:11, NIV

A solution came like a warm Chinook—completely unexpectedly. Donna's mom asked me to move in with them.

I was 15 and couldn't move out legally until I was 16, but knowing my escape was imminent—just 116 days away—I prepared, little by little. Donna and I began a stealth operation. Every day when I went to school I took an item of my belongings with me, and Donna put it in a box at her house. They were just small things—a letter, a book, a picture. I stuffed them under my clothes and walked them out of the house. In the meantime, her mom and dad were getting a room ready for us to share.

One morning I woke up thinking, *Don't take anything today.* My mother was standing at the front door. She searched my room every day and had become suspicious. She stripped me naked. "Where is all the stuff?" she screamed. I looked at her with a blank, wide-eyed stare and said nothing.

By the morning of my 16th birthday I had put the remainder of my things into two little boxes and hidden them in the garage.

It was snowing hard, and the snow was already more than a foot deep. Donna and her father were coming to pick me up in half an hour to go to live with them. I was so scared. I didn't know what Ingeborg would do. I thought she might grab and beat me till I was in a state where I couldn't walk.

I planned my escape. It was a Sunday morning. Close to the time they were coming I stashed the boxes in the snow and tiptoed to open all the doors slightly so I could bolt if I had to. As I walked back through the kitchen I noticed a gift for me next to the sour milk and mouldy bread—

an unwrapped pair of nylons. I picked up the nylons but without eating went back to my room and stood there in a cold sweat, my knees about to buckle and my heart racing. I felt so weak I could hardly move—like all energy had drained out of me. I thought I was going to throw up.

I waited till noon—the minute Donna was to arrive. I timed it so I could get down the driveway, jump in the car and take off. Otherwise, I thought, I might never get out of there. It was so hard and abnormal for me as a child to say *I'm leaving*, but I had to do it for my sanity and my life.

I looked at my watch, took a deep breath and felt my feet walking me to the family room, where Ingeborg and Helmut sat reading the paper. "It's my birthday!" I announced, to make sure they knew I was of legal age. "I want you to know I'm leaving today."

My mother raised her eyes from the paper. "What do you mean you're leaving?" Her tone was cold, but my stepfather was startled. When our eyes met, a great heaviness fell on his countenance. So much was written in his sadness. I saw he knew I had to leave to survive. I could almost hear his thoughts—*I'm so sorry for your suffering these seven years; what you have been through has been so wrong.*

I knew this man cared for me. He was kind but hadn't been allowed to show it. He was frozen—caught in Ingeborg's spell, and his deep remorse reached out to me in that momentary sorrow to say how much he regretted that he hadn't defended me.

"I'm moving out," I repeated. Ingeborg glowered. I think she was shocked. I stood waiting for them to say something, but they didn't. The words hung between us—the last words I spoke under their authority. I turned and left in silence.

Donna's father had arrived. He got out to help carry my two boxes, but Ingeborg had recovered sufficiently to appear at the door. "Get off my property! I'll sue you for trespassing," she screamed. "Get away now!"

Slightly perplexed, he hesitated, but he got back in the car and waited while I struggled through the snowdrifts with each box.

I got in the car. As it pulled away slowly, snow crunching under the tires, I looked back. The door to the ice princess's castle was now shut. Despite the horrors of what my life had been at Ingeborg's house, the departure was painful for me. I stared at the receding snow-covered cold and empty shell that should have been a home. What did I have to show for the years with my mother but bruises, unresolved conflict and the echo of her mocking voice in my memories? I was free from her abuse, but I wasn't free inside. A mixture of conflicting emotions churned in me. There was nothing to go back to. It was the end of a chapter. I could only go forward, and I didn't know what the future would bring.

UNDER THE INFLUENCE

I saw Ingeborg occasionally after that. Two weeks later, as I was waiting for the school bus, she drove by on her way to work. She glared at me and turned away as if I were a stranger. It felt like a stab to my heart.

No matter what a mother is like, a child always wants her love. I eventually learned how to fill that gaping wound with the love of God my Father. He gave me the mother-love she could never give.

When my grandparents learned I had moved out, they were very upset. They knew I didn't have money and were afraid I might end up on the street as a prostitute. I'm sure Ingeborg conjured some lies to make me look worse and increase their concerns. They didn't know the situation. That grieved me. They came to Canada immediately to see if they could influence me to go back to her house.

I desperately wanted to visit with my grandparents. I hadn't seen them for four years, but when Ingeborg found out they were coming, she took time off work to be at home and keep an eye on the situation. She still made every effort to keep us apart.

My grandparents, hoping to talk me into going back there to live, begged me to go to Ingeborg's for dinner one night. For their sake I consented, but I dreaded the thought of seeing her. I had only been away a couple of months.

Ingeborg knew I was coming. When it came time to sit down to eat, I was standing with Oma and Opa near the dining room table. I noticed, and pointed out to my grandparents, that there was no place setting for me. It hurt me deeply. I saw surprise and helplessness in their eyes. Then Opa, struggling for words, asked Ingeborg cautiously, "Uh...do you think we might have an extra plate and fork for Belma? I can get it. I'll set a place for her." He pulled up a chair for me between them.

The evening was torment. My grandparents tried so hard to convince me to move back. To every scenario they presented, I replied that I would do anything for them but not move back into my mother's house. Ingeborg shoved food into her mouth and said nothing. I cried throughout the whole dinner. It really saddened my grandparents, and it was painful to see them at such a loss. By the time Donna's father came to pick me up and we hugged goodbye, their grief had built a wall of separation between us. Like Ingeborg's husband, my dear grandparents had come under her spell. They were blinded and helpless in my mother's presence.

THE TRUTH

Knowing my grandparents were visiting, Donna's mom invited them for tea. A few days after the dinner they came to Donna's house to meet her parents and see where I lived. They hoped to convince Donna's parents to send me back to Ingeborg. Instead, a surprise met them.

They saw the room Donna's parents had built for Donna and me. They also heard from Donna's mom, who spoke some German, about the beatings, the abuse, the police, the Children's Aid and my situation at my mother's house. That was the first time they were exposed to the truth. I had tried to tell them previously but, not wishing for them to be distressed, had never shared details. They listened and cried. They were relieved that Donna's mom was so sweet. She promised to take care of me.

MY NEW LIFE

I lived with my adoptive sister, Donna, for about a year. I was expected to pay rent at her house, but I didn't have any money. When summer came I got up at four o'clock in the morning and caught a bus with all the Italians to a farm, where I picked strawberries. I had a big basket, and the more I picked, the more money I made. It was hard work and I made only $17.00 a day, but it felt good to be able to pay my own way.

My time with Donna was really colourful. We had a lot of fun together, but eventually she met a guy in school and got into drugs and parties. That changed our relationship. She wanted me to join in, and I couldn't. My grandparents' influence was too strong. Other than taking a few drinks while under her roof, I had the sense to stay away from drugs, boys and influences that could derail me. I had a single goal in mind. I wanted to finish school, graduate and become an airline stewardess so I could fly to Germany and see my grandparents.

ON THE STREET

Eventually Donna moved in with her boyfriend, and I was left in the house alone with her parents. With Donna gone, her father began making inappropriate advances toward me. Once he lured me into the back bedroom, saying, "Here—I've got some money I want to give you." He gave me the money and grabbed me. He held me close and wanted me to take my clothes off in return. He was strong, and it was all I could do to escape. I wasn't safe there anymore and felt forced to leave, but where could I go?

Two awkward weeks later I moved out with all my worldly possessions in one little backpack. It was the end of September. As hard as it was to give up a nice, warm bed, the alternative was unacceptable. I found myself on the street and homeless.

Every day for the next four months, while I was at school my mind was preoccupied with finding a house where I might stay that night. Who could I get close to so they would invite me home?

I stayed at school doing homework as long as I could. Then I said to someone, "My parents are working and can't pick me up until later tonight. Could I go to your place after school please?" I'd go home with them. Dinnertime rolled around. I'd say, "I guess my parents must be working late," so they invited me for supper. When my parents didn't arrive, I would sometimes be allowed to sleep on their couch, but they told their child that it was only for one night. The next day, I did it all over again with another family.

Once when I went home with somebody and bedtime came, her father said, "She's not staying here." They sent me on my way at eleven o'clock, and I had no place to go. I found an unlocked car, crawled in and slept in the back seat. Four months went by in a blur. No home and no food, but I managed to stay in school and keep studying.

Meanwhile, Donna arrived at school every day happy, completely stoned and oblivious to the realities of life. She went home every night with her boyfriend, to a roof over her head and a bed to sleep in.

By November the weather was turning cold. It was already snowing, and I was mostly sleeping in the back seats of cars and sometimes under trees. Evergreens were the warmest because their branches were low—almost touching the ground. With no mittens, my hands were cold. In the cafeteria people started noticing I didn't have food, and some shared their sandwiches with me. What would I do with winter coming?

HOPE AT LAST

One of my friends suggested a room for rent in a residential area just around the corner from the high school. Every day for two weeks during lunch hour I went there and knocked, but no one answered. Back and forth I walked past a man, who eventually asked where I was going. I told him.

"Go in there and talk to my wife," he offered. "We don't have a room to rent, but she might be able to help you."

I met his wife, Monika, and their kids: eight-month-old Connor and Kaliee, a four-year-old. We chatted. When it was time for me to leave, she asked me to come back again. The next day they had a proposal for me. They invited me to move in and sleep on their couch for free in exchange for babysitting their children every Friday and Saturday night while they went out.

I was so relieved! It was just before Christmas. After school that day I took my little backpack to their house and had dinner with them—a real meal! Then a glorious bath. I was in Heaven!

Every night I slept on the couch and loved it. It was wonderful to be somewhere where I wasn't wakened in the middle of the night by a woman standing over me ready to beat me.

Mike and Monika were a popular young couple in their twenties. She had blonde hair and a nice figure, and he was dark and good-looking. Their children loved me instantly, and I loved them. Friends were always dropping in, and they introduced me. "This is Belma," they said. "She's living with us now." The words were like hot milk and honey to my spirit. We all sat around their long table to eat, and I was always included. The amazing goodness of every kind word and gesture pierced my heart, and I absorbed it with a hunger I didn't know I had.

For five years, until I was 22, Mike and Monika's house was my home. They took absolutely no payment from me and didn't expect me to work. After I had struggled so hard to survive at Ingeborg's and Donna's, it was an enormous relief. They contacted Children's Aid, who came to see us at the house and committed $90 a month toward my living expenses. Mike and Monika gave me the money for books and necessities. They took me shopping and bought me clothes. Mike even took me to the mall and gave me money so I could get Monika a pair of socks as a gift to put under the tree at Christmas.

I felt safe at last! Mike and Monika were good to me and treated me like family. Eventually they even took me along camping to Wasaga Beach.

Mike was a family man of integrity. Never once did he make advances toward me. He was a good husband and father and great with his children. He came home from work and played with them. I pondered Mike's interactions with his kids, and I missed my dad. I watched and wondered, *So this is how children play with their dad when they are little. This is what it's like to have a dad!*

My life with my dad had been cut off beyond my first 26 months, and my experience with Opa fell short. Opa had been wonderful toward me and had loved me, but he was always busy and didn't really have time to play.

THE LOST YEARS

The first year I was with Mike and Monika, they helped me plan a trip to Germany to see my grandparents. Oma and Opa sent me tickets, and I went for the whole summer.

It was beyond wonderful to see my dear Oma and Opa again and to be back in the midst of familiar, happy sights and sounds of my beloved Germany. I breathed it in deeply. The feeling of being there was like healing oil that flowed throughout my spirit, soul and body—a therapeutic balm for my emotions and memories—but there was an edge to it. A tinge of sadness enveloped me.

I wanted to be little Belma again—the one who played in the garden, who fit in and belonged, but that little girl was gone—only a memory. Even though I reconnected with my cherished environment, change had eroded what used to be. The beatings had crushed me. Sorrow and the natural course of life had marked my grandparents. Too many unshared life-moments had passed us, making it impossible to go back to the family intimacy we once knew. I grieved the lost years. It was the same grief I eventually felt when I reconnected with my dad.

On the flight back to Canada, as I looked out the plane window I tried to sort out the jumble of feelings, experiences, memories and present circumstances in my mind. Even though I had just lived the fulfillment of a dream of 12 years, I couldn't shake the hollowness.

I thought about the lost years when I should have been surrounded by the comforts of home and familiar things.

My reminiscences that day, as I sat overlooking the unending expanse of ocean, formed a foundation for my present-day ministry with First Nations people. The chiefs of many tribes have granted me uncommon favour to visit their reservations and teach their people a form of dance that honours God. I have a connection in spirit with them. I understand the lost years they experienced when their children were brutally kidnapped and abandoned to the harsh world of residential schools. Just like in my life, their language and heritage were beaten out of them, and they weren't allowed to be themselves. Years later, when some of them did reconnect with their families, they returned to an environment much different than they remembered. Because we've shared similar pain in our hearts, I am able to understand them.

FAMILY LIFE

When I returned from Germany Mike and Monika were really excited, and I found out why. They had built me a bedroom in the basement—a room of my very own. It was beautiful! Carpeted floor, stucco walls, a bed, a dresser and pictures on the walls. It was private and had a door. Such a surprise! I couldn't stop hugging them.

What wonderful people they were! To this day I love them and respect them as family. Because of them I finished school and reconnected with my grandparents. They were most significant in helping reshape my life.

Now that I was in regular communication with my grandparents, whenever a letter came from Oma, Monika would be out on the street waving it as I came home from school. "Belma," she called, "there's a letter from your grandma!" She looked after me as if I were her daughter. She did my laundry every week. If my socks had holes in them, she said, "Look at these socks, Mike! We need to go buy her some socks."

The next summer I got a job at the Board of Education library. I was given a pile of books to read and summarize. It was a great job. I took the books home, read them and got paid while I sat in the backyard. I was with Mike and Monika all day and could help with the kids. As soon as I had an income, I tried to offer them some room and board, but they refused. They were more concerned about my well-being than about money.

Soon money wouldn't be a problem.

Chapter 6

From Runaway to Runway

Do not conform to the pattern of this world,
but be transformed by the renewing of your mind.
Then you will be able to test and approve what God's will is—his
good, pleasing and perfect will.

ROMANS 12:2, NIV

I was finally living a normal life, with normal people, free of every kind of worry. Never once did Mike and Monika imply that I was a burden to them. It was a world of acceptance and love. But something troubled me. I still felt an emptiness inside that I thought should have gone away. I was restless, always looking for something elusive that might fill me or make me whole. The same hollowness drove me to search for my dad. If I found him, I reasoned, it would go.

One day while I was walking in a mall, I was approached by a modelling agency. They offered me an opportunity for what they called a "radical upswing" in my life. I decided to give modelling a go, thinking it might fill that nagging void. Models have automatic recognition and attention, and I craved it. My unconscious sense was that modelling might give me all that my mom had denied me—love, acceptance, admiration, value and recognition. The possibilities excited me, and I signed up with the agency.

Modelling did fulfill some of its promises. I loved being pampered. People put nice clothes on me, fussed with my makeup, and took pretty pictures—all the things I had yearned for my mother to do. It worked for a while. The emptiness wasn't as pronounced, but when the novelty wore off, I saw a dark side to these material blessings.

My first modelling assignment was on a boat. I was to model bathing suits. "No thanks," I said. Modesty was deeply rooted in me. Inevitably, my time with that agency was short.

Despite the fact that the first agency didn't work out, modelling intrigued me, so I took a course in my hometown. Another agency solicited me, and I did a lot of runway work, fashion shows and photography sessions for newspapers and magazines. I became good friends with the director and, on her recommendation, approached an agency in Toronto.

The jobs were good. The money was good. The attention was good. I was in my own little world of fame and fortune. There was just one problem. The emptiness developed a desperate edge and became a black hole. Regardless of what I did, it consumed the joy and value of every achievement. It was swallowing my life faster and faster, and I knew something had to change.

THE MISTAKE

I was now in my 20s. Many of my friends had boyfriends and lived in common-law relationships, but I was still single. I wondered if marriage might fill the emptiness. Perhaps it would leave if I had a husband who loved me and I could love. Did I know what love was? Not really. But that didn't cross my mind.

I met Jack when I was around 17 years of age in high school. We didn't have a deep connection. He was kind to me. He thought I was beautiful and liked being with me. He had a car, and that was attractive to me as a teenager. He introduced me to his family, and I really enjoyed spending time with them on weekends. His mom was loving and interested in me as a person.

Jack and I were together for a long time. By the time the friends around us were getting married, we had been dating for four years. With thoughts of a lasting relationship on my mind, I suggested we consider marriage. He agreed. It seemed the natural thing to do. We designed the ring, and the jeweller slipped it on my finger. Within a few months I was walking down the aisle.

As a child I had seen the church around the corner from my grandparents' store hold weddings. Every Saturday I ran there to watch the bride arrive in her processional, often by horse and buggy. I had always imagined I would have a "royal" wedding like that, but it didn't turn out that way. We had a big wedding with all his relatives in attendance, but I had only Oma, Opa, and my few friends.

Something else troubled me. I was very unhappy going into this marriage. It didn't feel right.

What a mistake! Just like my dad, I married for the wrong reasons. I had thought the emptiness would leave if I got married. Instead, it grew teeth. It felt like a monster that was devouring me. I didn't realize I had taken a man into my life because I needed a father figure. I thought a husband would meet my needs and resolve my emptiness, but a man can't fill that void. Had I known more about God at the time, I would have known that God didn't design men to do that. He especially didn't create them to give women what they need from a father.

REUNION

Had I been patient and not rushed into marriage I would have found the father I was yearning for. The same year I got married, my father flew to Germany and at the Frankfurt airport searched a phone book for the address of every person whose last name was the same as my grandparents. He mailed each one a registered letter requiring those who accepted it to sign for it.

All the letters were returned unopened except one. He knew that letter had reached my grandparents. He sent a second letter to them with one attached for me. He asked my grandparents to forward it.

I was calling my grandparents regularly by this time, and one day Oma said, "Your father is looking for you." She told me about the letter.

I waited anxiously for it. The little girl in me responded. The thought of being in my daddy's presence made me feel like a princess—special, precious and loved. The longing I had in my heart to connect with him would soon be fulfilled. I was overwhelmed that he was searching for me. I would see him face to face, and no one would be able to tear us apart again.

When the letter arrived, something in my life shifted. I stood at the mailbox trembling, holding it, drinking in the writing on the envelope. I ripped off one end, unfolded the paper and absorbed the words: "My dear Belma. Please write to me German or English or you may call me in my store. Love your Daddy."

My Daddy! He wanted me to call! I had wondered how I might react at this moment, but I hadn't anticipated being nervous and afraid. What would I say? What would he say? Would he still love me? Would he be proud of me? Would he be happy about the way I'd grown? Did he know how my mom treated me? Would he be upset about me leaving her? And my husband—would he like him?

A few days later I called. "Hello, is this Mr. Ejubowic?"

"Yes, this is he." I didn't even notice what his voice was like. My heart was racing and the thought consumed me that I was actually speaking to my real father.

"This is your daughter, Belma." I paused, not knowing what to say.

Suddenly a dam burst. "When can I come see you?" I blurted, shocking myself. My anxiety had turned to fury. "Why didn't you find me before this?"...*When I so desperately needed you,* I added in my thoughts. My chin began to tremble violently, and tears spurted from my eyes as though they had been capped and could no longer resist the pressure.

"Come and see me and I will explain everything," he said gently.

My father owned a men's clothing store, and I drove there the following Saturday. I arrived at 11 a.m. but had to give myself a moment before I could see him. There was a restaurant across from his store. I ducked in there to collect myself and peer through the window to see if I could catch a glimpse of him. When I summoned the courage, I ventured over.

I opened the door, and there he was. I recognized him instantly. Tall, with dark hair; his eyes—welcoming, friendly—looked familiar to me. He wore a three-piece suit, and the photos I had seen of him at my grandparents' home came to life. I felt suspended in a moment outside of time. I was little Belma again looking at him, and he was the most handsome man I had ever seen.

He recognized me. He was smiling. He walked toward me, and I walked toward him. There seemed to be air under my feet. The floor had lost its substance. I couldn't speak.

When we reached each other, he took both my hands and looked into my eyes. "You're just as beautiful as I knew you would be."

Still holding my hand, he led me behind the desk and cash register and opened a drawer. He pulled out a brown envelope and tipped it, and hundreds of pictures fell on the counter—me as a baby, he and my mother, my grandparents, my relatives, the garden where I grew up in Germany. "These will prove that I'm really your father," he said.

Had he doubted that I would believe who he was? It hadn't crossed my mind. He pulled out another brown envelope. "Before you read these court documents about what your mother did, I want you to promise me one thing: that you will always honour and respect her. She carried you and brought you into this world. Because of her, you have life."

At that moment he didn't know the depth of grace his request would require, but I couldn't refuse.

DADDY

We spent the rest of the day looking at pictures and talking about what happened when I was taken from him. We talked about the lost years and filled in the gaps. He asked me about my grandparents and told me he had remarried and had two children. I found out I had a half-brother, Derin, four, and half-sister, Sera, thirteen. He had given Sera the middle name *Belma* and said he needed to tell his wife and children that he had found me.

It seemed like energy from his heart flared toward me, encompassed me and exploded in me. I felt deeply connected. I couldn't stop repeating to myself, *My daddy is sitting in front of me,* and I stared at him in wonder.

Our first hours together passed in a moment—a bittersweet reunion of great joy and deep sadness from knowing we could never recover the 19 years we had been apart. In the months that followed we struggled to find something that could replace them, but we learned over time that nothing could.

After our meeting my father called my grandparents to thank them for sending me his letter. Once when he was at my house, Oma called and spoke to him. "It wasn't my fault," she said. "I'm so sorry. We didn't force Belma to stay in Germany with us all those years; we just wanted to help."

"I don't hold anything against you," Dad said. He forgave and let go of the pain he suffered in my absence.

I met often with my dad after that. Each visit was filled with joy and restoration. As much as my relationship with him grew and flourished, another was disintegrating. My marriage was very empty, and emotionally I was wrecked.

FALSE EXPECTATIONS

Jack and I felt disconnected. Neither of us knew how to be married. We didn't cherish each other, and we both felt hurt, rejected and robbed. I've omitted the stories of the pain I experienced because I want to respect and honour his parents and family. I can, however, share my contribution to the relationship.

I heaped my unresolved issues on him and expected him to fix my life, but he couldn't. I also couldn't accept him for who he was. Judgmental and critical, I always put him down. I resented him for not being the person I wanted him to be, and for not healing the heart of the little girl that I still was on the inside. I did to him what my mother had done to me.

I know now that our behaviour toward each other was a result of the abuse, "baggage" and unhealed "stuff" from our dysfunctional backgrounds. Had we been healed, we could have had a chance at a great marriage.

The story of our marriage is a book in itself. Like so many who find themselves in a predicament similar to ours, we tried to build on a foundation of sand.

Eventually I received the healing I needed through God, and I forgave Jack. I pray he might find the freedom of forgiveness too.

TROUBLE IN THE FAST LANE

To compensate for my failing marriage, I became increasingly involved in runway modelling, magazine photography and commercials. I always did well until an agency required me to remove my clothes. Because I refused, I had to keep changing agencies.

One day I was sent on a movie audition. If I got the part, I would make $40,000. My agent told me the movie company would provide an outfit for me. I arrived at the audition and found a rack with skimpy little pieces of fabric on it. In the boardroom next door, the producers and directors were waiting for me around a conference table. I was to enter the boardroom wearing the supplied "outfit." I called my agent. "There's no outfit here."

"Yes, there is," she said. "It's on a rack."

I was perplexed. "But there's no outfit on the rack. I just see little bits of material here."

"That's the outfit," she assured me.

We argued. There was no way I would wear a few bits of fabric for an audition. "I'm not selling my body!" I told her. Her perspective was different. "We hired you to sell your body. That's your job, and it's worth $40,000! Do it!"

I was tired of being pressured to conform to worldly standards and made to feel like a fool for my choices. Apparently if everyone was doing it, it was right. Not in my life!

I quit and walked out confidently, my head held high, but where was I going? Where was my life going? I had questions, and no answers. As I walked away, a warm rush flooded my body, and I knew I had done the right thing. Oma would have been proud of me.

Another agency interviewed me, and I told them my story. "That's disgusting!" said the sympathetic representative. "We'll take you on." They arranged for me to audition for a brand-name department store catalogue. It turned out to be for undergarment modelling. "I can't do that," I said. "I'm a model. I model clothes, not my body." Again I walked out.

After all the hopes, dreams and energy I invested in modelling, it seemed like another unfulfilling dead-end. I was about to give up, but I received a call from an exclusive Toronto agency. To protect their privacy, I will call it the Jay Summer Agency. My friend Janet worked for them and made very good money.

I was required to appear for a "go-see" at a warehouse. It was a dodgy place, and I felt uncomfortable, but I let it pass. I walked up a big stairway, and as I reached the top I saw on a wall a giant poster of Janet as a Playboy centrefold. The earlier discomfort turned sinister. A tangible darkness engulfed me. I shivered. I didn't know at the time that Jay Summer sent all her girls to the Playboy Corporation.

The moment I saw the poster, I walked down the stairs and out the door.

Later that day, back at the agency, I sat waiting to be called for another interview. I was to meet Jay Summer, the owner. She didn't show. I was invited back the following week to meet her and sign the contract.

The next week when I met Jay I wanted to recoil. Her eyes were thin, shiny slits like those of an angry cat. They looked evil. I learned later she was high on drugs.

She cased me out, eying me up and down to check out my worth. She liked me. I tried to buy time. I told her I would consider working with her agency and would return Monday to sign the contract. In reality there was a battle going on inside me: to sign or not to sign. In my thoughts I cried out, *Oh God, I'm scared!*

What was I getting into? I knew inside it wasn't anything good. I called my friend Donna. "If I did something really bad, would you still be my friend?" I asked.

I called Oma and asked her the same.

They were both puzzled but said yes. Neither had any idea how bad a thing I was about to do; nor did I.

That night an exceptional thing happened. In a mini-vision I caught a flash of myself as one of Jay Summer's "girl toys." I saw myself sliding down a muddy tunnel with no ability to stop. I knew what it meant. That's what would happen to me if I signed the contract. I would be trapped and my moral values compromised.

I was in the valley of decision.

Pause and Reflect

God has a plan and purpose for each of us. Until we know God's purpose, we may feel empty inside. We search and try to find purpose in many things: relationships, careers, hobbies, music, entertainment, various religions and systems of philosophy—anything to fill the "hole" that exists deep inside because we don't know why God put us here on earth. Until we give up our own efforts and seek God for the purpose He planted in us, we scramble around in futility, trying to find out who we are supposed to be.

Identify your heart's desires.

How have you built your life around your heart's desires?

Is your life purpose something to achieve, or is it something that flows out of who you are?

Do you think God created us to do a task or to be in relationship with people, or a bit of both?

Belma's experience is a great example of the importance of a father in the life of a young girl. So many young women make the same mistake Belma did. Lacking proper fathering, they marry, expecting the man to fill a father's role, or they look for love in all the wrong places. This is a strong call to fathers to involve themselves in their daughters' lives and give them the love, support, guidance and affirmation they need to move forward positively.

Name some men who have shown you what a father should be like.

Would you say that the role of father has been filled or is lacking in your life?

Is it possible for God to step in, be your Father, and re-parent you?

Our past experiences can create expectations of how we should be treated, and unconsciously we teach people to treat us that way. Belma's expectations had been severely affected by her experience with her mother, and when she experienced deprivation in her marriage, it seemed normal. She subconsciously expected it.

As we realize who we are in Christ, we can learn to expect respect in our relationships. When we require respect from people, they are more likely to give it.

God wants to heal our hearts of past hurts and teach us healthy ways of relating to one another.

Do you respect yourself?

Do you require others to respect you? Why or why not?

Chapter 7

Breaking Down the Walls

And they cried out in a loud voice:
"Salvation belongs to our God, who sits on the throne,
and to the Lamb."

REVELATION 7:10, NIV

I was 25, and my life was unravelling. Inside I felt frantic. My marriage was failing. I was about to make a pact with the devil to sign my life away. I started to feel there was no point in going on.

My deadline was fast approaching. In two days I would sign the contract with Jay Summer, but that afternoon Donna came to my door. Her mom had died six months earlier, and she had descended into deep despair. She and her dad had both been on the verge of suicide because her mom had meant everything to them—the centre of their world. But now here was Donna, beaming!

"*What* happened *to you?*" I blurted.

"I found the Lord," she said, grinning from ear to ear. I felt like I was looking at some cheesy act in a two-bit movie.

I laughed and rolled my eyes. "Oh brother! You've got to be kidding!" Even if she wasn't joking, she was too good a friend to send packing.

It was great to see her. I invited her in, and we went for a swim in our pool. As we floated on air mattresses, I found out she was serious about finding "the Lord."

"What do you mean you *'found the Lord'?*" I mocked her. It sounded ridiculous.

Donna rolled off the mattress and dove underwater because I was making fun of her. When she surfaced, I stifled a snicker. "Wait a minute," I asked. "What about me? Why can't I *'find the Lord'?*"

"I'm not going to continue this conversation. If you really want to know what it's all about, come with me someplace Saturday night," she said.

The radical change in Donna piqued my interest. Out of curiosity, I agreed to go.

Changing Lanes

That night, August 13, 1983, Donna took me to someone's house. I found out it was called a house-church. We arrived a little late. At a glance I realized I looked a little different from the others in the room in my black nail polish and black leathers.

The room was small but packed with about 20 people standing between rows of chairs, singing with their hands raised. We made our way to the only empty seats, in the front row.

When everyone sat down, a young guy with rows of gold necklaces stepped forward. Donna said he was the preacher. He talked about God's love and about Jesus being "the same yesterday, today and forever." It was the first time I heard that God loved me and that I was not a mistake. Then he talked about healing and asked if anyone needed to be healed. A 74-year-old lady with a cane hobbled forward. She sat down near me on a chair and extended her legs. One was shorter than the other. The preacher put his hands up and prayed in a foreign language. I later learned that this practice is called "speaking in tongues." He didn't touch her, but her short leg visibly grew longer than the other one.

"My goodness, Donna," I gasped, "the short leg is too long now! What'll they do? Will they push it back?"

No one had to "fix" it. Both legs evened up. The woman got up, left her cane at the front and walked back to her seat without a limp.

Another woman came forward. She was from Trinidad. The pastor prayed for her, and she fell on the floor right in front of me. I took a step back and stared wide-eyed. If that wasn't enough, the preacher continued to pray for an evil spirit to come out of her. They called it "deliverance." She was as close to me as my feet, and I saw what was going on. She became agitated and screamed. Her eyes turned red, and she foamed at the mouth and threw up on the floor. Rather than being frightened or repulsed, I was fascinated.

Then, as I watched, something happened to me. I saw a vision of a blanket coming down and settling on her. It was a blanket of peace. In a moment her hair-raising screams stopped and she lay in perfect peace.

That's what I need—right there! Something good had happened to her when she fell to the floor, and I wanted to be on the floor with her so I could have it too. I stepped over her to reach the pastor.

I gave the pastor a long list of prayer requests. At the same time, a prayer formed in my own heart. *Lord, kill me!* I begged. *I don't want to be the same as I have been anymore.*

If Jesus can make a leg grow and give that woman peace, I thought, *He can kill me.* I really wanted to "die" and give Jesus control of my life.

I didn't know I was asking for something in agreement with Scripture. The Bible says we must "die" to ourselves, give our lives to Christ and allow Him to take over. That's what I wanted. My life was out of control. Some unseen, dark force was driving me in the wrong direction.

Suddenly I too was on the floor and I was stuck to it. I couldn't get up! As I lay there I had a vision. It was like seeing a movie. I saw thousands of pieces of broken glass. God's hand swept across the pieces, and they all came together, forming a glass heart. I heard a voice say, "I'm going to turn your stony heart into a heart of flesh." With these words it seemed like a bucket of fresh, bubbly water dumped on me and flushed my whole system. I was washed clean!

The pastor spoke again, and I liked what he was saying, but he kept interrupting himself with goofy phrases like "Praise the Lord!" "Thank You, Jesus!" "Hallelujah!" The interruptions were annoying. I noticed something else new. "The Holy Spirit? What's that?" I asked. I had a lot to learn, and Donna tried to explain. "Anytime you want to talk more about the Lord or the Holy Spirit, just call me."

OUT OF CONTROL

I had a great time. I fell into bed that night and had a rock-solid sleep. In the morning when I awoke I still felt good. I was tingling all over as if my whole body was on fire. Out of my mouth popped the words "Praise the Lord!" I was shocked. I slapped a hand over my mouth. I was used to swearing, not using words like "Praise the Lord"!

"Well, never mind," I said to myself. "Thank You, Jesus!" The words burst from my mouth so unexpectedly I jumped out of bed as if something in it had made me say them.

I rushed to the bathroom and stared into the mirror to see what had happened. The reflection appeared normal. Then I looked at my hands and heard a voice say, "These hands will praise Me."

Whoa! I thought. *That's the Lord talking to me!*

I went downstairs and pulled out the toaster. "Thank You, Lord, for the toaster," I exclaimed. I couldn't contain it. Was Jesus now in control of my mouth? "Hallelujah for this knife! Thank You, Lord, for the butter and my toast." Everything was, "Thank You! Thank You! Thank You!"

Three hours later I realized the emptiness inside that had consumed me was gone. I was so full, I was about to explode. Then I remembered a song I had heard the night before:

Are you washed in the blood—
In the soul-cleansing blood of the Lamb?
Are your garments spotless? Are they white as snow?
Are you washed in the blood of the Lamb?

I sang that chorus over, and over, and over. After a while the song changed. Now I was singing, "I am washed, in the blood, in the soul-cleansing blood of the Lamb." I started moving my arms and hands with the music. *What am I doing?* I thought. *If people saw me doing this, they would think I've lost it.* I closed the drapes.

I couldn't stop singing. Different movements came as I sang. Then it occurred to me, *Jesus is talking to me through movement, and I'm talking to Him. This is my love expression to Him. It's my communication with Him.* With each movement I reached higher and higher toward and into God. Suddenly I felt lifted up physically, as if onto a platform. I was in Heaven in God's throne room. The Lord was there, and He was so happy, He was crying. His tears rolled down and covered me.

I had a rich time with the Lord that day. Donna had loaned me a Bible. I opened it to a passage that said, "Praise him with the timbrel" (Psalm 150:4, KJV). I didn't have a timbrel. *I'll just use a frying pan,* I thought. I tried to do everything I read in Scripture.

I came across a Scripture on baptism, so I filled my bathtub and dunked under. "There, Jesus," I said as I got out. "What next?" I just kept reading and doing.

Literally, I was transformed overnight. I met the Lord and ran into His arms, because it was the first "forever" safe place I had found. Joy at finding safety caused me to express my love for God, not just from my heart or with words but with my body as well. The movement developed into deep intimacy with Him through dance.

NO REMORSE

For the next three years I danced in my private worship to the Lord. It was such a personal expression of my love for God that I couldn't imagine telling anyone about it.

I had finally found the place where I belonged, the place where I fit. I plugged in quickly because I gave myself fully to God in worship right away. I believe God wants everyone to know that in the midst of terrible circumstances He is there for all who call on His name.

I never imagined He would call me to a ministry of teaching worship dance. I didn't even know what worship dance was, but the thing that came most naturally to me turned out to be my life's purpose—one I would never have discovered had I not chosen to turn my life over to Him.

So many changes took place in me at the same time: I took off my black nail polish, purged my closet of all the immodest and black leather clothing I had started wearing in the previous couple of years, and lost my taste for secular music. I couldn't get enough of Christian music albums, and I couldn't wait for church again the following Saturday.

Monday came, and Donna gave me my own Bible. I was so excited! I wasn't at all the same person who was supposed to sign with Jay Summer's agency that day. I called Jay and said, "I'm sorry, but I won't be working for you."

"You can't do that!" she exclaimed. "You promised to sign a contract with us."

"I've changed my mind," I responded with no remorse. My priorities had changed. Jesus, and transformation in Him, took first place.

I called my agent friend at the local modelling agency and told her what happened. She was upset. "You could have really gone places," she lamented, but then—she came to church with me and accepted the Lord herself. After that she supported me because she understood my decision.

I had been making good money modelling, but I decided to give it up. I wasn't destitute. I had managed to save some cash to carry me over.

POWER OF LOVE

Rather than concern myself with money, I wanted to share Jesus with my family. I especially longed for my mother to be set free. I told Donna I had decided to go and see her, but Donna was very apprehensive. She begged and pleaded with me not to go. "Why are you doing this?" she asked. She wanted to call the police. She was sure my mother would pull a knife and kill me because of how demonized she was. I told her I felt compelled to go because I didn't want my mother to be separated from God for eternity.

I got to Ingeborg's house. She opened the door and greeted me with reserve. "Mom, I have something very important to tell you," I said. "Can I come in?"

She motioned me in, and we sat across from each other at the kitchen table. For 45 minutes, I explained what had happened to me. Tidal waves of God's love washed over us throughout that time. She stared at me, eyes wide, and for the first time I saw into her soul. Tears coursed down her cheeks. She hadn't cried from the time she was a child.

"I'm telling you this, Mom, because I want you in Heaven." She let me pray with her, and I felt her heart soften as she cried. I felt peace, and it assured me: mission accomplished!

I got up to leave and hugged her. She received my affection—something she had never done.

Unfortunately, after this occasion Ingeborg gave no indication of wanting to grow in the Lord or in knowledge of His Word. Our relationship didn't grow either. She remained *verklempt*—German for "very closed."

A year after I came to know Jesus, my grandparents came to visit and stayed at my mother's house. I went to see them, but my mother mocked me. "Belma's a Jesus Freak," she scoffed. "Don't talk to her!" She wanted nothing to do with me. Opa agreed with her and joined in the mocking. It was really discouraging, but I saw in Oma's eyes that she and I were connecting. She looked sad. I had a chance to share with her privately that she needed to give her life to Jesus so she could spend eternity in Heaven. She understood and believed my words. It gave me great hope.

Only when I committed my life to Jesus did I develop peace in my relationship with my earthly dad. When the order was right—heavenly

Father first, then my earthly father—I could accept and embrace life as it was and be content in my relationship with him.

Without a Christian background it was very difficult for my dad to understand my faith. He once asked, "How can there be a trinity? Three in one?"

God gave me the words: "Dad, when you got married you were a husband. Then you became a father. You also had a career as a tailor. There you go! You were three in one just like God!" His eyes grew wide, and I knew he had received a revelation. I smiled. "See, Dad? You understand."

There was a time when I was to appear as a guest on the *100 Huntley Street* Christian television program. I called my dad while I was getting my makeup done. "I'm going to be on TV today. Watch it, Dad, because I'll be talking about you."

He was excited. "What channel?" he asked.

"I don't know! Just keep flipping till you see me."

I told my story on the program and said to the viewing audience, "I'd like you to get on your knees and ask Jesus to come into your heart."

When I got to my dad's house after the program, he had lunch ready, and we sat down. "Let's thank God for this food," he said. It took me aback. He had never talked like that. "What's going on?" I asked. "You never pray."

"You told people to get on their knees and pray, so I did," he said with a smile. His eyes sparkled!

I could see that my father had a new understanding. It was real. I could hardly talk.

Next I wanted to share with Oma. The opportunity came.

When I was 30, my beloved Oma was taken to the hospital. I called and asked the nurses to bring her to the phone. "Oma," I said, "let's make sure you asked Jesus into your heart. Let's pray right now."

"Yes, yes, yes!" she said, and she sounded happy.

As I was driving the next day, I had an open vision of my grandfather sitting on his bed weeping inconsolably. I heard him sobbing, "I can't go on without her." A heaviness came over me as if I was right there with him.

DEAREST OMA

A month later I went home for lunch from the Christian daycare centre where I worked. A letter was in the mailbox. It was a generic notice that informs a person of the death of a loved one. It stated the location and time of death and where they were buried.

My dear Oma, who had been a mother to me, had died the day after we spoke. At the time of her passing, I had seen the vision of Opa weeping. She was buried before I knew she had died. Ingeborg, who was in Germany at the time, hadn't told me until the funeral was over.

Again I was a victim of Ingeborg's cruelty. She knew Oma was Mom to me, and she chose not to inform me of her death and burial. I was devastated not to have attended Oma's funeral.

When I got back to work I was so distraught the director told me to take some time to recover in the next room. I wept for five hours. Suddenly it was as if the room around me vanished, and I was in another place, looking at a little window. The curtains were parted, and there was Oma. She wore a white gown and was moving easily and freely. She appeared to be pain-free. That was amazing to me because arthritis had given her extreme pain and poor mobility in her later years. The Father was holding her hand on one side, and Jesus on the other. The Holy Spirit was moving through her. She said, "Belma, I know now why you dance. He is so worthy to be praised." Then the curtains closed, and I knew she was in Heaven. I had peace.

REACHING OPA

Ten months later Oma's neighbour contacted me to tell me Opa was on his deathbed. I felt an urgency to see him and share Christ with him because he hadn't believed the last time we had been together. He needed to go to Heaven too. In my hurry to get to Germany, all I took was my Bible.

"Opa!" I cried when I walked into his hospital room.

He saw me, stretched his arms toward me and screamed my name. It hurts me to remember the desperation in his voice. I ran toward him, but he covered his eyes and shrieked, "The light! The light is so bright!"

"Okay," I said, "I'll turn off the light." I flicked off the switch and walked toward him again, but the closer I got, the more he cried that the light was too bright. Then it dawned on me. The light he saw was coming from inside me. It was the light of Christ in me.

It was heartbreaking for me to see him absolutely helpless in diapers. He couldn't do anything for himself. He took Oma's picture from the nightstand and shook his head, gasping between deep sobs, "I can't live without her." I tried through my tears to console him. "Oma is in Heaven," I said. "I want to tell you about Jesus."

"No, no," he said. "You can't! They're all waiting for me!"

"Who is waiting for you?"

"Look," he said, his eyes wide with alarm. "Look in the corner! The demons—they're all waiting for me. They're waiting to take me."

He was seeing in the spirit realm. "No! They won't take you," I insisted, but he had given up.

"Yes. I've done too many bad things in my life."

"It doesn't matter. All you have to do is pray with me and they won't take you."

"No! No! They will!"

CALCULATED EVIL

That's what I encountered every day for three weeks. Every day we had the same conversation, but he wouldn't pray with me.

Then suddenly one day, Ingeborg walked into the hospital room. She had heard that I was in Germany and immediately flew over. For me to be there was the last thing she wanted. I didn't know it then, but she had an agenda, and to bring it to pass, she needed me gone. She introduced chaos to accomplish it.

Ingeborg was on one side of Opa's bed, and I was on the other. She leered at me and snarled, "What are you doing here? You have no business being here." She swore at me and called me names.

"Stop!" Opa cried. "That's my granddaughter. Don't talk to her like that! It's wrong!" He had pneumonia and was very sick. It took all the energy he had to speak.

My heart broke that Ingeborg could be so cruel to me in front of Opa. But her behaviour wasn't random madness. Her moves were calculated. She aimed to be as mean as possible. She spit at me across his bed and sneered, "You should never have been born. You were a mistake!"

"You can say anything you want, but don't hurt my grandfather," I countered. That didn't do any good. She came around the side of the bed and kicked me. Opa, alarmed, tried to protect me and with what energy remained managed to utter, "Belma, get out! Get out! Leave here so she can't hurt you!"

I had no choice. I had to leave. Ingeborg must have been smiling at that moment. I found out later, that's exactly what she wanted. She absolutely did not want me there at Opa's death.

I walked down the street crying. Before long I heard someone weeping next to me. I looked to my right. It was Jesus—a transparent white figure walking with me, weeping. A tenderness, softness and compassion emanated from Him.

I went back to the house where I was staying with Christian friends, who prayed with me. Undone from being at my grandfather's bedside with my mother, I felt physically nauseous, extremely sad and grieved. That night I had a dream.

The dream woke me, and I sat with a start out of a deep sleep. Jesus was standing at the foot of my bed with His arms open and stretched toward me. I extended my arms toward Him and heard Him say, "The way you are reaching out to Me right now is the way your grandfather will reach out to Me with his last breath. Well done, My faithful daughter. I am God, and only I will see the end result."

A blanket of peace settled over me and through me, and I fell asleep.

That happened in October 1990, a momentous time not only for Opa but for Germany and for me. It was exactly the same time that Berlin was set free.

GOD OPENED THE WALL

While I was there the Berlin Wall came down. Along with the people, I was caught up in the mix of emotions and frenzied joy too long suppressed. The day after the wall fell was declared a holiday in Berlin. Balloons decorated buses, and rides were free. It was a weekday, but people flooded the churches to celebrate. My friends and I joined the celebration and packed into a church along with the masses. There wasn't a breath of room between us.

People were in a daze. They flooded in from the east. Some had walked five or six hours to get there. You could tell the ones from the east—their clothes were drab and greyish from being washed with dirt instead of soap over the years because soap had not been available.

At the church we watched a video on the events that happened the night the wall went up in 1961. So many of us had been there. Everyone was crying.

Then the video showed the opening of the wall that had just happened. Overcome with awe, one of the musicians jumped from his seat, ran to the stage, and exclaimed, "God opened the wall! God opened the wall!" Grabbing his trumpet, he lifted it to his lips and uttered a jubilant blast toward Heaven.

Inspired by the call, the drummer jumped from his seat, bounded onto the stage and joined the trumpet's proclamation of the glorious defeat of oppression with a triumphant drum roll. People joined in as they played, chanting through their tears, "God opened the wall! God opened the wall!"

Thanksgiving poured out to God in song, and we swayed left to right, left to right, gently at first, then with growing vigour. We were so tightly packed that when one swayed, so did all 600. Suddenly we swayed so hard to the left, the weight of our bodies flung the door outward, and we spilled onto the street. Some of us had a chance to grab flags before we tumbled out the door into a processional.

People gathered in the street and hung over their balconies, watching us march through Berlin, leaping for joy, waving our flags and repeating, "God opened the wall! God opened the wall!" Tears flowed freely.

It was surreal. What were the chances that I would have been there both when it went up and when it came down? It was no coincidence. I find that God allows me to see the beginnings and endings of significant events in my life to give me closure and to show me His finished work.

I never saw Opa again. It was so hard for me to fly back to Canada. I really had to release him into the hands of the Lord, but I knew he would be fine. After his "graduation" I had a vision of him in Heaven. He was with the Lord, fully committed to Him, holding His hands. No more struggling. He was in total peace, and so was I.

During that hospital visit I saw my mother alive for the last time. The next time I was in her presence—19 years later—I was required to identify her body after her death. I wish I could say that ended her influence in my life, but it didn't.

Pause and Reflect

Belma faced a critical crossroads in her life. Not only her eternity but her entire life on earth depended on this choice: Would she choose fame and the glitz and glamour the enemy offered, or would she choose God's path for her life? We all face that question: will we choose the world's way or God's way?

Which path are you choosing right now?

Can you explain why you are on that path or what brought you to it?

Do you need to make a change in your life choices?

Belma's mother needed deliverance and healing. Trauma and abuse create patterns in a person's life unless the person is redeemed and healed. I believe that Ingeborg made it to Heaven. Once a person commits their life to God, God holds on to them. He doesn't let go of His people very easily. Although Ingeborg didn't walk out her journey with God on earth, she gave God permission to save her by praying with Belma.

Are there people in your life who need to be "saved"?

Can you tell them about God's redemptive power and offer to pray with them?

Rejoice, for God is ready to help them—even at their last breath.

Beginnings

TOP LEFT | My mother as a little girl growing up in Germany. • TOP RIGHT | In the garden harvesting the grapes—my great-grandfather in the chair, my mother holding the garden rakes, and to her right, Oma and Opa.

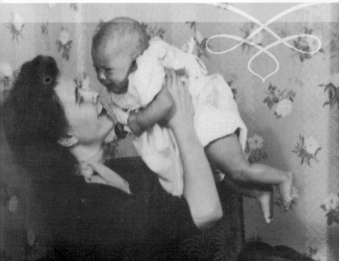

CENTRE LEFT | My mother and father on their wedding day.

CENTRE RIGHT | My father in Germany with Purzel on his lap.

BOTTOM LEFT | My mother holding me as a baby—a tearful moment!

P LEFT | On my mother's lap, posing for the camera. • TOP RIGHT | From left to right: my her, Oma, my mother and Opa. (Photo taken the first time my father went to Germany to meet grandparents and family.)

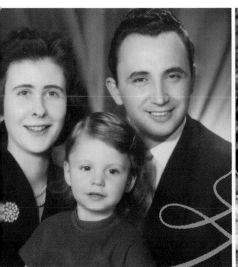

CENTRE LEFT | Our last photograph together as a family—Mom, Dad and me.

CENTRE RIGHT | Playing in the garden with my dolls.

BOTTOM LEFT | My kindergarten class—I am in the centre wearing suspenders.

TOP LEFT | Dear Oma and Opa on their wedding day! • TOP RIGHT | Oma, Opa and me sitting in one of our garden chairs. • BOTTOM | Watering flowers in the garden—life in the garden with Oma and Opa was safe while the world around me was in turmoil.

Life in the garden.

P LEFT | Carefree days riding my tricycle. • TOP CENTRE | Taking flowers from the garden
our relatives—wearing a favourite dress. (My great-grandmother made all of my clothes.)
P RIGHT | Here I am playing with Purzel. • MID LEFT | In Germany, children receive a
hultüte (a paper or plastic bag in the form of a cone) on their first day of school. It is presented by
rents or grandparents, prettily decorated and filled with toys, chocolate, candies, school supplies
d various other goodies. It is given to children to make this anxiously awaited first day of school
ittle bit sweeter. • MID CENTRE | The gate to enter the garden. • MID RIGHT | At the end of
e walkway was the little house we slept in. • BOTTOM LEFT | Looking through the pillars of the
andenburg Gate into East Berlin. • BOTTOM RIGHT | Soldiers in East Berlin.

Meine liebe Behna,
Bitte schreib mir
Deutsch, oder Englisch
oder kannst mir
telefonieren in
mein Geschäft.
Viele herzliche Grüsse
Dein Vatti

My dear Behna.
Please write to me
German or English,
or you may call
me in my store.
Love
your Daddy.

My teen years

FAR LEFT | My dad's letter that changed my life forever (written in both German and English)!

CENTRE | Leaning on a tree located in the woods that I was dragged off to and beaten.

TOP LEFT | Seventeen—living at Mike and Monika's place.

TOP RIGHT | Sweet sixteen—living at Donna's house.

BOTTOM | Oma and Opa meeting Mike and Monika (from left to right: Monika, Connor, Mike, Kaliee, Oma and Opa).

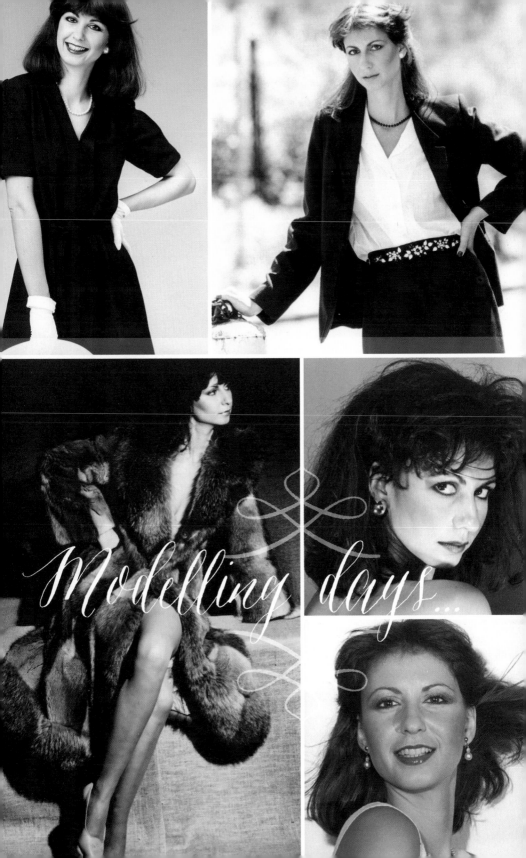

Modelling days...

Faith, freedom
and
dance...

TOP LEFT | While I was dancing at a conference, as my dress billowed around me, a lady watching saw her deceased grandchildren in the dress, lying in the arms of Jesus. • TOP CENTRE | An illustration entitled *Jesus and the Lamb,* by Katherine Brown. This picture got me through my first Christmas alone. It happened to arrive in the mail on Christmas Eve. • TOP RIGHT | With my dance teacher Karen Christian at a church in France.

CENTRE TOP LEFT | With my talented friends Grace (left) and Colleen (right). • CENTRE LEFT | In a studio recording songs for *Celebration of Dance* CD. • BOTTOM LEFT | Touring in New York City with Grace, Carmon (our producer) and Colleen. • CENTRE RIGHT | Photo shoot for the *Dance into Battle* video project. • BOTTOM CENTRE | In makeup for the video production *Dancing with God.* • BOTTOM RIGHT | Filming *Dancing with God* at Crossroads Television Studios.

TOP LEFT | Instructing children at a Mennonite church in Kitchener. • TOP CENTRE | Studio filmin for my first project, *Biblical Basis for the Celebration of Dance* (1993). • TOP RIGHT | Presenting flower dance together with a troupe of dancers in a cathedral in France.

CENTRE LEFT | Reading the Bible and spending time in prayer with the children in preparation fc the *Let's Dance* video production. • CENTRE RIGHT | Jumping for joy with the children during th location video shoot of *Let's Dance* at Lowville Park, Ontario. • BOTTOM LEFT AND RIGHT | Enjoyin every moment, the children leap into action for the filming of *Let's Dance*.

TOP LEFT | The children's dance troupe that travelled with me for ten years.
TOP RIGHT | After many hours of rehearsals, the dance troupe is ready for the filming
Biblical Basis for the Celebration of Dance.

Let's dance!

CENTRE LEFT | A scene during the filming of *Dance into Battle* with Catch The Fire School
Ministry. • CENTRE | Filming *Breakout* with German youth in Weinstadt, Germany.
CENTRE RIGHT | Production photographer Roland Senkel, working with producer-director
Marjonneke, during the filming of *Breakout,* while German youth look on. • BOTTOM | African
tent church where the youth were struck by the Holy Spirit.

Dance Into Battle (1997)—an exciting project based on the concept of spiritual warfare, filmed in many locations around Southern Ontario.

An exceptional collaborator, director of photography and cameraman, John Elder, from Crossroads TV Studios, filmed at least eight of my dance productions, including *Dance Into Battle*.

During the filming, powerful purebred Arabian horses were used to represent the body of Christ. Medieval Times in Toronto provided our production with the main character's horse and the rider. Our performers included actors, dancers and musicians from the International School of Ministry, representing many nations.

Producer-director Marjonneke, our drummer, Nuno Marques, and me unwinding during a break in the production of *Dance into Battle*.

"You have turned my mourning into joyful dancing. You have taken away my clothes of mourning and clothed me with joy."

PSALM 30:11, NLT

BOTTOM LEFT | My good friend, TV personality Moira Brown, directed a number of productions with m
BOTTOM CENTRE | My good friends Lorne and Doris Shepherd. • BOTTOM RIGHT | Daddy and me.

Chapter 8

Surprising God Encounters

*"And I will show wonders in the heavens above
and signs on the earth below."*

ACTS 2:19, ESV

I loved to worship the Lord in movement until His presence filled the room. For three years, with curtains drawn, I soaked in that heavenly atmosphere in the privacy of my living room. During that time, at a Christian concert I met Colleen, a worship leader at Meadowvale Christian Reformed Church near Toronto. One day while talking to her, I mentioned my unusual style of worship with body movement. I called it "my thing." I explained that this creative expression was a part of how I communicated with the Lord. She seemed interested and said she would drop by to observe. That was fine with me. "It doesn't matter when," I offered. "I do this movement expression all the time."

She came that evening at seven o'clock. When I explained I did this movement to music, she sat down at the piano and played all evening. But the movement didn't come. Finally, at ten o'clock she stood up. "Well, nothing's happening here," she announced, and she left.

I was curious. "Holy Spirit, why, when You move through me every day, didn't You move through me when she was here?"

He answered right away. "I don't want you to tell Me when to move. I want to be the One who inspires you to move." I accepted what He said and was satisfied.

At the same time my personal life was in turmoil. Our marriage had almost run aground. My church was struggling, and it eventually closed down. I had no clue how to move forward.

ALONE

My husband and I separated formally after ten years of marriage and two years later divorced. By the time he left, I was stripped of my money and all I had. I was alone again, a companion of rejection, abandonment and judgment. With the broken marriage came sadness and disappointment.

Unresolved issues from my childhood resurfaced to expose every painful wound of the past that I had not yet resolved. I was an unhealed angry woman, and I identified with Isaiah's words "storm-tossed and not comforted" (Isaiah 54:11, ESV). Yet through it all I clung to Jesus—a steady point of reference in the tempest. I needed His wisdom.

A CHRISTMAS MIRACLE

Christmas was coming, and I was by myself. No family and no fellowship. I wondered how I would make it through the holidays. One day I snuck into the back of a church and knelt with my face buried in my arms on the pew in front of me. I wept from the depth of my soul. I felt broken.

Through my tears I turned my head to the side. On the wall beside me was the famous drawing of Jesus holding a lamb on His shoulder. Suddenly I was in that picture. I was the lamb! The painting penetrated the core of my heart, and I had to get a copy of it. I needed it to undergird my very existence. I needed it now!

I phoned the church to ask if they knew where I could get the picture. They said it had been painted by an artist in the United States. With some effort, someone found the phone number of the artist's brother, who lived in a different state.

I phoned the brother and explained my mission. It didn't matter to me how I sounded. "I need it," I told him. "I'm not going to make it otherwise." I cried, begging him to contact his sister, and asked him to write down my address.

On Christmas Eve morning, at 11:30, my doorbell rang. It was the mailman. He handed me a tube with the print inside. The artist's number was with it, and I called her immediately.

She said, "Listen to this. My brother told me about your desperation. I had one print left to give away. I took it to the post office but had no money to mail it. I had no idea how I was going to do this. As I was walking—no word of a lie—a $20 bill came floating down from the air. It landed right in front of me. I picked it up and kept walking to the post office. The picture cost $7 to mail, and I had $13 left over. I went to the store and bought three turkey TV dinners so my children and I could have Christmas dinner. Without it, we wouldn't have had any food!"

A Christmas miracle! And it wasn't just for me! The print is still hanging framed in my office.

Why Me, God?

I didn't go to a church for eight months. Everyone had abandoned me, and I felt judged. WDCX Radio and Trinity TV Broadcasting Network became my "church." Oddly enough, in those eight months, I grew much closer to the Lord. He was my shepherd, and I was His lamb.

Eventually I joined Meadowvale, a wonderful, loving, family-oriented church, but I was still reeling at the loss of my marriage. Because of my grief I couldn't bear for anyone to talk to me. I wanted to be left alone.

"Don't go to the phone; go to the throne!" That's the advice I once heard from a wise woman of God, and that's what I did. I always went to the throne, because I had no one to turn to but God. I felt like only He could understand my pain.

It was painful for me to go to church and see happy families together. My family was destroyed, and I was angry at God. I remember swearing and railing at Him, asking, "Why did You let this happen?" After I had released my anger I was very upset with myself, but regardless of how angry I got, I always talked to Him.

During those years, I added angry letters to my outbursts at God. No one saw them. After I released my anger on paper, I repented through rivers of tears and wrote God love letters. Sometimes I danced out my anger and pain. I learned the dance of lament and the dance of grief. I now teach these as therapy movement for the release of pain.

Life was horrible in those days. I sat and watched the clock. Some people watch the clock wondering how they'll make it through the next hour or the next day. I had to make it through the next minute. The pain was so great, but its effect multiplied because I couldn't sleep at night from distress. The doctor gave me sleeping pills, and I remember looking at the bottle, thinking, *If I took those pills, I could end everything.*

MY BEST FRIEND

One night I was reading the book *Welcome Holy Spirit*. I remember saying out loud, "Holy Spirit, I want You to be my best friend." I was alone in the house, and I found that a bit scary, so I pulled the covers over my head and added, "But can You come in the morning instead, please? Don't come tonight."

The next morning, I was sitting at the kitchen table watching the birds outside. They were jumping around in circles. *They look like they're dancing,* I thought. Suddenly I was startled to feel two hands grasp my cheeks and turn my head. In the doorway stood a tall white figure with eyes of love. He walked toward me. As He walked, a cloud-like substance remained wherever He had been. I stood up momentarily. He sat down beside me at the table. When He sat down, I sat down, and the white substance surrounded me. The distance between me and Him was like the space between the soft white membrane under an eggshell and its hard exterior. That spiritual membrane fit around my whole being like a glove. I looked in His eyes, and He spoke to me with them.

I had been confused about many things, and He gave me clear direction for my future. I remember saying, "Let Your will be done, Lord." For three days after that, His wonderful presence, in the form of the white cloud and peace, lingered with me.

During these difficult days, God was faithful and met me in many ways. When I began attending Meadowvale Church, one elder, Joe, always came to say good morning and give me a hug. He never asked how I was and didn't need me to say anything. That kind of understanding brought little bits of healing to my heart and meant more to me than he will ever know.

I loved the solid, meaty teaching at Meadowvale. I understood it. I really enjoyed the pastor's focus on worship every Sunday night. Every message was rich with God's Word, and I was hungry to learn. I ate it up.

One Sunday morning I was sitting in church feeling broken and thinking, *Jesus, all I want today is a hug.* Again two hands took my cheeks and turned my head toward the back of the church. I noticed a four-year-old boy sitting on his mother's lap. At that instant he jumped off and ran all the way across the church to me. He looked into my face and said, "I came to give you a hug."

All I saw were his precious eyes. Jesus was looking at me through them. I extended my arms toward him, and he hugged me. I felt a rush come into my body through him. It was a strengthening from the Lord. An impartation. He held me and hugged me with all his might. Then he released me and jumped back. "I have to go back to my mommy now," he said, and he ran away.

The child ran back across the church, and I sat stunned at my encounter with God. *"Lord Jesus, You gave me a hug!"* I marvelled. What an experience! After that it didn't matter if the minister preached or not. God was with me! I basked in His glorious presence.

It has taken many years, but I now see the Lord as my husband. When I speak at singles' conferences I'm very aware that everyone seems to want a mate. We have to surrender that desire to Him and be satisfied with Him alone. That realization opened many doors for me.

Pause and Reflect

The rejection Belma felt from her mother, right from the womb, was no doubt one of the roots of her rejection of her husband and his rejection of her. Rejection has cycles, but there are ways to break them.

We all feel rejection at points in our lives. Have you suffered the pain of rejection by a loved one?

Are there times when you continue the cycle of rejection by your treatment of others?

What steps can you take to find healing and truth in Christ?

Chapter 9

Commissioned

"My presence will go with you."

EXODUS 33:14, ESV

Colleen invited me and four others to a worship conference in New Orleans, to observe and learn. Five thousand people were registered. We had never been to anything of that magnitude.

Before the meeting began, people throughout the audience were playing musical instruments at their seats. When I asked somebody why they were doing this, the person replied, "We just want to praise the Lord, and Scripture tells us to praise Him with our instruments."

It occurred to me: my body is my instrument! I can praise Him with my body! It was a revelation.

I liked the anonymity of that huge gathering. It was easy to be free and be myself. I decided to go to the back of the hall and do "my creative expression" with Jesus.

At the back people lined the wall. That puzzled me, but what happened when the music started unravelled me. They all began worshipping with the same creative expression that I had experienced for three years in my alone time with God. *That's exactly what I do at home!* I thought, and I had imagined I was the only one in the world doing it!

I ran to find Colleen and exclaimed, "Look! They're all doing 'my thing'!"

"Oh Belma!" she said with a smile. "That's dance!"

I was bewildered. "That's not dance. That's relationship with Jesus. My love expression to Him!" I didn't think she understood, and I didn't wish to pursue it, so I made my way back to the others along the wall.

It was beautiful! Everyone along the wall was worshipping. I thought I'd entered Heaven! The beauty of their movement was a river of refreshing to my soul. I soaked it up.

OUT OF THE CLOSET

I was lost in God's presence when the music stopped abruptly. The worship leader, Kent Henry, spoke into the microphone. "The Lord just told me to stop the service because there's a woman here who God gifted three years ago with something she calls her 'thing.' She's been hiding it in her worship closet for three years. The Lord says, will that woman come forward please? He wants to pop that cork tonight!'"

The words burned through me. *That's me*! I looked at people around me but suddenly felt very shy and afraid to move.

Another woman walked forward and stepped in front of Kent Henry. He glanced at her momentarily. "You're not the one," he said. "She's back there," and he pointed directly at me.

My body started trembling, and my feet moved on their own. They walked me up the aisle. I was crying when I reached the stage, and when Kent Henry prayed for me, something happened inside. I felt like I floated back to my seat, carried on God's hand.

As I settled in next to my friends Colleen and Grace, the worship team broke into songs of warfare. An inexplicable urge to dance seized me. I was in such a hurry to get out of the row that in one leap I jumped over two chairs and into the aisle. For the first time I worshipped with movement in public.

Colleen and Grace both were itinerate worship leaders among Christian Reformed churches. They were amazed. "Wherever did you learn to do that?" one asked.

"That's what I called 'my thing' with Jesus," I said.

They immediately invited me to travel with them as their principal dancer. In an instant I graduated from the "closet" to the stage because God had commissioned me.

Travelling with Colleen and Grace was a wonderful experience. We were a worship team of 30 that ministered in Christian Reformed churches. As part of the team I worshipped with movement, sometimes with flags. I danced up and down the aisles while they performed and sang. It was a glorious time for me and a great joy to inspire others with the gift that had inspired me.

HUNGRY FOR GOD

At home in Meadowvale, children appeared to be especially receptive to movement with worship, and I sensed God telling me to launch a children's dance workshop. I prepared a plan, and the elders accepted it. Thirty-eight children registered for the first six-week course. When the six weeks ended, I offered the class again. This time twelve came. These twelve became a dance troupe that remained with me for ten years.

Ages four to six, they came once a week for a one-and-a-half-hour class. They loved the Bible teaching and worship dance so much that they asked to extend the class to three hours. Then five. Then a full day! Many brought lunch or dinner so we could stay together.

We had a wonderful time praying, worshipping and ministering to the Lord. I taught them God's Word because of their hunger for the Lord. They became filled with the Spirit and started praying in tongues. God gave them visions and prophetic words. Often we only danced the last 45 minutes and spent the rest of the time reading Scripture and learning how to talk to God. They often shared private things that happened in their homes, and we prayed over them. No one ever repeated our confidential conversations or prayers to anyone outside our circle.

Sometimes the children brought pictures of their families to a gathering, and we prayed for them. If a child was in distress, we invited him or her into the centre of our circle, laid hands on them and prayed. When parents came to pick up their children, they sometimes commented, "Who was here? I feel God's presence."

The children loved our all-day gatherings. They grew in intimacy with God, and out of their relationship with Him they danced in worship. Then, about two years into our training, we were asked to put on a presentation at an arts conference in a nearby city. I cupped my hands and said to the children, "When we are in our classes all day, we are really in God's hands. It becomes a platform for the day. That platform is just being moved to a different place, so we're safe." The children weren't in the least nervous. When they stood before the audience, their focus was on the Lord. They danced to Him.

The response was profound. People wept, overcome by God's presence in worship.

The next thing we knew, we were invited to dance at a gathering at Copps Coliseum in Hamilton. The children were in awe because they had never experienced an event of this magnitude. We practiced choreographed dances, and they marched out like a little army, waving their flags. They focused on the Lord even though their faces appeared on the jumbotron.

Thousands came, and for the first time the children experienced what it might feel like to be a VIP. Because of the crowds, we were assigned security. Each child had their wrist tied to a rope so we couldn't be separated as we wove our way through the crowd. After they danced we were inundated with admiration for the excellence of their performance and with booking requests. Mostly people wanted to know what steps I had taken for them to be so steeped in God's glory.

As the children's dance troupe became known, so did this ministry. People began giving me money for my work, so I needed to formalize the ministry with a name and bank account. My grandparents had given me some money, which I had tucked away, sensing that I was to reserve it for the special purpose of setting up the ministry to which God had called me.

PEOPLE'S CHOICE

He even named the ministry! At first I called it Crystal Waters Music in reference to Revelation 22, which speaks of crystal waters flowing from God's throne. It seemed appropriate because God's anointing flowed in my workshops, and people were touched and transformed by the Lord. When they became free, we always danced to celebrate. The celebration of dance had such a great impact on people that I began receiving random cheques made out to "Celebration of Dance." It recurred with such frequency that the bank suggested, "Let's add the name 'Celebration of Dance' to the business rather than sending back cheques to be rewritten to 'Crystal Waters Music.'" *Celebration of Dance* became the people's choice for a name.

It is a wonder how God works through us for His kingdom purposes when we yield to Him. The ministry He had given me flourished, and I could see God's favour and blessing operating in my life.

Chapter 10

Learning to Follow

All these blessings will come on you
and accompany you if you obey the LORD your God.

DEUTERONOMY 28:2, NIV

In 1989 a Christian Reformed church in a nearby city invited me to teach their children. I wanted to play fast music, bring out the flags and make it exciting. When I asked the Lord what I should teach, He said, "Teach them about prayer." *Prayer! They'll be bored just sitting around talking about prayer,* I argued.

"I want you to teach them about prayer," God repeated.

I settled the children, six to nine years old, in a circle and asked, "Who has a hurt in their heart today?" Every hand went up.

"Okay then," I continued, "Let's take the hurts and with our hands give them to Jesus."

I showed the children movements to make and played a recorded song about 58 seconds long. When we finished, the children were crying. That's not what I expected. I wondered what had happened. One little girl said, "When we were down like this," she placed her hands on the floor, "I felt something on both my hands. I opened my eyes and saw Jesus' feet on my hands. I felt something go through my hands and through my whole body, and now I feel better!" Her face beamed.

Another little girl said, "I saw Jesus coming from that corner over there," she pointed across the room, "and He had a big knife in His hand. When He got to me, I gave Him my heart and He cut out all the pain and hurts. Then He gave me my heart back, and now I have no pain."

More children jumped up. "Jesus came to me with a big scrub brush," said one. "I gave Him my heart, and He scrubbed it and gave it back to me. Now I feel all clean."

"He brought me a blanket of peace and put it over me. I feel good," chimed in another.

One by one, each child gave a testimony about what had happened to them during the song. They were very excited and wanted to do it again.

An hour and a half went by. I didn't have a chance to teach them dance. We read Scripture and prayed till it was time to leave. On my drive home I was concerned about the next class because the church was paying me to teach dance, and we hadn't danced.

The following week I went early, bracing for complaints. The kids and parents came early too, but the kids had their Bibles. I hadn't told them to bring those.

The parents waiting to talk to me looked like a reception line. I took a deep breath. They wanted to know what had happened in the previous class. "My son Johnny came home, cleaned his room and picked up his socks," said one mom. "He has never done that before, and there's something different about him."

"My little girl is talking to Jesus all day long," said another.

Parent after parent testified about a change in their child's behaviour as a result of the first class.

"All I can say is that God met every child where they were at," I told them. "He ministered to them in whatever way they needed." The parents were grateful, and I had thought they were about to fire me!

On this day the children and I sat down in a circle, and I said, "Let's read some Scriptures." We read Psalms.

Then spontaneously, one by one, each child stood up, turned outward and lifted their arms in a movement of praise until a beautiful circle of worship formed. "What are you doing?" I asked one little girl.

"I hear a song in Heaven," she said.

I talked to several other children, and it seemed they were all hearing the same song. I watched in awe the physical manifestation of God "inhabiting the praises of His people" displayed before me through these children. In response to the Holy Spirit, they were worshipping with movement on their own without my instruction and without audible music. All we had done was read Scripture and pray.

GOD'S PROGRAM

The minister heard what God had done and asked if we would do a 20-minute presentation for the congregation. The children were delighted. The day of our event we ended our presentation with the 58-second song through which Jesus healed the children's hearts. The children finished in a worshipful face-down position on the floor.

In a Christian Reformed church, the order of service is very structured, with a timed and precise schedule. But as we ended, we heard the clicking of shoes on the hardwood floor walking forward from the back of the gym. It was the father of one of the children, who had been doing sound for us. I thought maybe something was wrong, but when he got to the front he faced the church and said, "I watched my son dance up here with such freedom, and I want to do that. I'm trying to imagine what it's like to be so free and move like that, but I'm so bound up I can't do it." His eyes filled with tears. "Can somebody here please help me?"

The children still remained on the floor in their closing position. I looked at the pastor, thinking, *This is not part of the program. What am I supposed to do?* I was a little alarmed, thinking, *I don't want to get fired!*

One by one several men stood to testify of the impact the children's dance had on them.

Then the dike broke and the boundaries of the programmed service disintegrated. The whole church erupted with people standing and commenting. Many women and youth asked, "Can she come and teach us?"

I was invited back to this church to teach men, women, children and youth. In fact, this booking launched the ministry. The news of what happened spread like a brush fire, regionally, provincially and nationally. People called from other churches, and suddenly I was in demand and travelling all over the world, teaching worship dance.

For more than 10 years the group of children I first taught at our church travelled with me to conferences. Eventually they reached an age when they moved on with their lives—went to university, developed careers or got married—but throughout their years of ministry, they took it very seriously. They had to be on time for rehearsals. If they were late, they didn't dance, and everybody was always on time—except once.

KNIT TOGETHER BY LOVE

At that time we were participating in a big event at a local church. Organizers expected 5,000 people. The stage consisted of five tiers, and we had to be organized, sharp and coordinated. Lisa, our lead on the top tier, was late.

We were ready to start rehearsal, and no Lisa. Everyone knew she wouldn't be allowed to dance even if she showed up. It didn't matter that she was the lead. That was the rule.

Twenty minutes into the rehearsal the door opened, and there was Lisa's father.

"I just heard God tell me to put her in," I told the kids. "I have to do it by faith," They understood because they were getting used to hearing God's voice. "Lisa," I said, "take your position."

Lisa's father approached me and handed me a folded paper. "This afternoon my wife told me in front of Lisa that she is leaving me," he said. "While we argued, Lisa kept saying she couldn't be late for rehearsal. She begged us to bring her even though she was in the middle of the news of our breakup. I rushed her here. I'm really sorry we're late. This is the letter my wife wrote me."

I thanked him for telling me and for bringing her. When Lisa saw him talking to me, she ran up to us in tears and asked me to tell the kids.

We went into the prayer room, and I told them. The kids started wailing and weeping. We had 45 minutes before our performance, and we hadn't eaten supper. We were to join the event's leadership team to eat, but we couldn't. I sent a note of apology, explaining we had had an emergency and asking if someone could send food in for us.

We cried, ate, wiped our faces and went out to perform. Lisa was in front. She danced, her head held high, and she was beaming—radiant in spite of her pain. The Holy Spirit danced through her. When we left the stage, we went back to our room and cried again.

Those kids understood ministry. They were deeply connected with each other and with God. They knew they had to be anointed to minister through dance. They knew the Holy Spirit would empower them and minister through them if they did what they were supposed to do. They also knew they could cry and be themselves behind closed doors.

What if I hadn't heard God or hadn't obeyed Him? What if I had refused to let Lisa dance because she broke a rule? She might have been wounded for life or felt rejected. The incident reminded me how important it is for us to spend time alone with God because then we recognize His voice in critical times.

GOD'S ORDER

When I was first teaching this group at my home church, we were together all summer, three to five times a week. We grew close because we shared spiritual things, such as lots of prayer. Some of these children were featured in my first video, *Biblical Basis for Celebration of Dance*. And then one day the Lord told me to stop teaching them. I was shocked. I couldn't believe what I was hearing, but I knew God's voice. Then He showed me the reason.

He said clearly that the kids idolized me and had elevated me above their parents. I knew that was wrong. God wanted it to stop. It was hard for me, but I obeyed and told the parents what the Lord had said. Then I went home and cried.

Interestingly, His communication with me didn't end there. "Now I want you to teach a workshop to the moms of the kids," He instructed. Another surprise!

I called the parents back and invited the moms to a workshop. Every mom came. I taught them everything I had taught their kids, and more. They learned the differences between presentational dance, devotional dance and congregational dance.

When the moms went home, the children were excited that they had spent the day with me. They wanted to know what happened.

When the children heard what their moms had learned, the children could no longer feel superior to them. The moms were now just as knowledgeable. They could teach their children dances, and the children could look to their mothers the way they had previously looked to me. The mothers and children had great fun dancing together in worship that evening. When the dads came home, the kids invited them to join in. Now whole families were dancing together at home. I marvelled at what God was doing.

The next day at church the worship team played a song I had taught the moms. The children got excited, and little circles formed of family members dancing together in worship.

Proper order had returned. The Lord said to me, "Okay, you can start teaching the children again."

It humbled me to realize that out of my obedience to stop teaching the children new life came to families and to our church—new life I could never have orchestrated myself. Nobody could take the glory but the Lord Himself.

It was wonderful to see God at work in our church, but right around that time God also began to manifest His presence in a very unique way among the churches worldwide.

Pause and Reflect

We want to learn how to recognize God's voice so we can be obedient in challenging times. Our prayer always has to be "Lord, help me stay close to You. Holy Spirit, don't let me get away with anything."

Is there something that God has asked you to do that you have not done yet?

Could this be a good time to do it?

Ask the Lord for courage and strength to be obedient!

Sometimes when God uses leaders in powerful ways, others idolize and praise them instead of God. Some leaders enjoy the attention and purposefully operate to receive praise. They love the fruit of their work more than they love the Lord. They become impressed with their own ministries and see themselves as the centre of the work and as the focus of glory.

Our main goal is for God's will and purpose to be fulfilled. When God entrusts ministry to you, you need to foster and steward it. You need to make sure it fulfills His purpose. That is a huge responsibility. You have to hear His voice and lead people in the direction He wants them to go.

Can you think of ministries that were caught up in fame or riches, began to detract from God's glory, and sullied the reputation of the church?

What eventually happened to those ministries?

Chapter 11

"More, Lord!"

That you may be filled with all the fullness of God.

EPHESIANS 3:19, ESV

Beginning in 1994 people travelled from all over the world to a church called Toronto Airport Christian Fellowship (TACF), now known as Catch the Fire Toronto, to experience what was called the "Toronto Blessing." The blessing started late in January that year when during an ordinary church service God surprised everyone and "showed up" in a way no one expected. God's presence, in the form of His Holy Spirit, was so powerful that, from all reports, lives were radically transformed.

People's reactions when the Holy Spirit came upon them attracted the most attention. They responded to God's touch and presence on their physical bodies in a variety of unfamiliar and unusual ways. Many reacted with loud laughter, crying, shaking, spontaneous dancing, shouting and various vocal expressions. Some found these behaviours, or "physical manifestations," difficult to explain and accept. I had my introduction to this "phenomenon" early on when it was just beginning.

One Sunday afternoon I accompanied a friend to the Airport church to drop off a letter. When we arrived, an unexpected sight greeted us. The church service was definitely over, but people were rolling on the floor, laughing hysterically. I sat down at the back of the church, watched and kept my distance. While I was hungry for more of God, I was highly skeptical of all the unusual activities. *This can't be for real*, I thought. *These people are looking for attention.*

Then I noticed Pastor Carol Arnott rolling on the floor laughing with everyone else. I was appalled! How undignified! I was critical, skeptical and glad I didn't belong to "this weird church." It was an understatement to say that what I was witnessing didn't fit my Christian Reformed grid.

As I stood near the door ready to leave, someone came and asked if I wanted prayer. *I can always use prayer,* I reasoned and quickly added,

I'll receive whatever You have for me, Lord. What is not of You, don't let it come on me.

As soon as I agreed, out of nowhere ten people surrounded me to pray. As they prayed, I felt heat penetrate my face, as if the Lord's face was right against mine. His love filled me from the bottom of my feet up through my whole body.

I am by nature analytical and don't accept anything readily without checking it out first, but that prayer time was such a good experience, I decided to go back and observe a meeting.

During the months that followed, I went every night to observe. I was fascinated by it all but not totally convinced it was of God. While I didn't experience any of the physical manifestations, I noticed, in my quiet times with the Lord, changes in my attitude and in the way I related to people. I forgave others with greater freedom and was more aware of times when I needed to repent. I also noticed a growing desire to know God more intimately. As these changes took place in me, I concluded that what I was witnessing at TACF was indeed a move of God, and I became more open and receptive.

I shared my experience with my friend Sandra and talked about some of the deep changes that had taken place in my heart. She agreed to go with me but was concerned that some of the manifestations might happen to her. "Nothing will happen to you," I assured her. "I've been going for weeks, and nothing has happened to me. You'll be safe."

TICKLED ON THE INSIDE

As usual, the worship was wonderful. When it was time for the announcements, I noticed that a friend on my left was making strange noises and jerking slightly. It looked like he was trying to contain laughter. I had never seen him act like this before, and he seemed embarrassed. I pointed him out to Sandra, and he surprised us both by exploding in hysterics.

All of a sudden it seemed the heavens opened and a bucket of laughter dumped on the two of us at the same time. We burst out in uncontrollable laughter. It overwhelmed us. The more we tried to stop, the more we laughed. Sandra fell over sideways, and I slumped on her with my head on her hip—so unladylike for someone as proper as I am. Completely uncharacteristic! We tried to sit up and regain our composure, but as soon as we did, we fell over again. I held on to a chair to pull myself up and landed on the floor between two rows of seats.

Sandra, in a laughing frenzy, tried to get away from me. Every time we touched, it set us off even more. It felt like we were being tickled on the inside. We were very loud. Someone was speaking on the platform, but we couldn't hear him. We were having our own little party.

At the end of the evening we crawled out the door on our hands and knees, not at all embarrassed, and not caring how we looked or sounded. It was quite normal to leave this way.

The next morning I awoke full of God's presence—refreshed, rejuvenated and deeper in love with my heavenly Father.

That evening Sandra and I went back. This time we wore ski pants. Before the meeting I said to the Lord, "Whatever it takes to change me and make me more like You, I am open. I'm Yours." The pastor asked me to share what God had done the night before. When I opened my mouth to speak, no words came out. I tried for about five minutes, then the laughter started again. The ministry team prayed for me, and I fell to the floor without anyone touching me.

A WALK IN THE RIVER

As I lay on the floor a beautiful presence flooded me. For three hours my physical body was unable to get up. As I "rested" there, in my spirit I seemed to be walking in a lush green pasture hand in hand with Jesus. We came to a river. He said it was the river of life that flows from the throne of God (see Revelation 22:1). The first part of the river was very shallow, about a foot deep. As we walked further in, I noticed the water flowing through my leg, not around it. Going deeper, refreshing flowed through my body from my toes up to my head.

That night I awoke suddenly at two o'clock in the morning. "Look at your leg," I heard God say.

Since July 1988, I had had a chronic skin condition on my leg. It started as a mild rash, but by March 1994 it covered a four-by-two-inch area and was swollen about a sixteenth of an inch. It was extremely irritating, itchy and painful. I had been to the doctor many times to seek treatment, but he told me I would have to live with it. I looked at my leg, and the rash was totally gone! I gasped and touched the spot, rubbing it in awe. My leg had smooth brand-new skin. I wondered for a moment if I was dreaming. I asked, "Where did it go, Lord? What happened?" Eventually, I fell back to sleep.

When I awoke that morning, l immediately remembered my shock and awe during the night and looked at my leg first thing. It hadn't been a dream. My leg was still healed. It was very hard for my brain to process. I wondered that God loved me so much He would heal me.

Since then I have learned that healing doesn't depend on how much God loves us. He loves us all the time and with infinite love. Rather, healing depends on what Jesus did on our behalf. He was whipped until His flesh was in shreds and His bones were exposed, and with those "stripes" (Isaiah 53:5, KJV), the Bible says, He took all our "pain" (Isaiah 53:4, NIV) and "sicknesses" (Matthew 8:17, NLT) and gave us His divine health and healing. I now believe that we don't have to pray for healing. Healing is already ours if we believe that Jesus is the Son of God and gave Himself for our salvation. I think we just have to receive it.

That night I had a related dream. In it I relived my previous night's experience of walking hand in hand with the Lord in Heaven. This time when we came to the river, He said, "This is the river of life. In it there is healing. As we walked through it, you were healed. My child, I love you; receive My love." Even in my sleep I was overcome. I woke up weeping, feeling overwhelmed with gratitude.

Later I made an appointment for my doctor to look at my leg. The nurse checked my chart. Over the years I had been given many prescriptions for a medicated cream. Both the doctor and the nurse marvelled, saying I was very "lucky" because such skin conditions don't go away. They asked what had happened. I told them God had healed me. "I believe you, Belma," the nurse said. "I feel a stirring inside like something exciting is about to happen. Like the medical and spiritual are coming together as one!"

I left the doctor's office thanking the Lord for His presence and for a chance to share my testimony. I still thank Him for His grace and mercy toward me and give Him the glory.

GOING DEEPER

Because of the unusual and unexpected things I experience with God, I have dropped all expectations of what can or should happen in times I spend with Him. I just allow myself to be drawn into Jesus' presence. Since those days I have not had any other physical manifestations, but God's work in my heart has led me into deep repentance. God meets me where I am.

My love for the Lord grows every day. I find I have greater trust in Him and a deeper understanding of how much He loves me. I have a renewed passion to read His Word. I want to lose sight of myself and be completely surrendered to Him. I want His substance, His presence, His strength, His agenda and His purpose for my life. Like a bride in love with her bridegroom, I keep falling in love with Jesus again and again.

As I surrender and submit to Him, allowing Him to mould me, He refills my empty heart and covers me with His power and glory. In my time alone with Him, He refreshes and energizes me, and I say with joy, "I know that whatever God does lasts forever; there is no adding to it, no taking away. And he has done it all in such a way that everyone must feel awe in his presence" (Ecclesiastes 3:14, REB).

I continued to go to revival meetings at TACF, wanting to be in the middle of what God was doing. Seeing Him work in such profound ways in people's lives was glorious and fulfilling. I couldn't stay away. I didn't want to miss anything. Those years were among the most exciting of my life.

But then, over time, something changed in my heart. People around me were experiencing tremendous moves of God, and I began feeling left out. I prayed and prayed, but I didn't sense Him doing something grand in me anymore.

"What is wrong with me?" I asked God. "Why aren't You touching me? Have You forgotten me?" I continued to go to meetings, watched, waited and wondered.

One evening during worship I hung my head and prayed in my heavenly language. Suddenly I felt something that I can only describe as liquid heat rising inside. Despite the music and singing, I heard God's loud whisper, "I want you to worship Me. Seek Me."

IN HIS PRESENCE

That night I discovered another facet of what it means to meet God face to face. I raised my hands, and His presence wrapped around me. I repented for seeking a manifestation rather than seeking Him. I enjoyed a powerful time of intimacy with Him.

The next day I was shopping but very conscious of God's presence. As I walked through a department store I prayed quietly under my breath, thanking the Lord for the intimate time of worship the previous night. I realized I had wandered into the store's baby section. Wherever I looked I saw Barbie dolls, stuffed kittens and action figures. This was the department I generally avoided because it served as a painful reminder of my own childless marriage. I wanted to run but instead found myself glued to the floor. I stood silently, looking around. Something was different. I realized my heart wasn't reeling! The deep ache I had carried for seven long years was gone. I gasped at the wonder.

I stood glued to the floor, thanking and praising Him. Joy bubbled up inside, and my spirit cried out, *Lord, I want only to follow You and receive what You have for me.* The familiar liquid heat poured over me and filled me with peace.

I had never been healed from the devastating revelation that my husband was having a baby with another woman. In my mind it should have been my baby. My pain ran deep, and anger turned to dark depression. Anxiety-filled days gave way to lonely nights and endless hours of weeping. Bitterness was entrenched in me. When I found out they were having another child, I came very close to a nervous breakdown.

Until this moment I had shuddered whenever his girlfriend, Noreen, came to my mind. I was tormented for almost six years and always had a hard time in toy stores and around baby things. They all stirred up bitterness too difficult to bear.

NOREEN

Some days passed. Once while I was having devotions and praying in the Spirit, I was prompted to pray for Noreen. That shocked me, but I felt a love and compassion for her that I knew could only have been from the

Lord. As I prayed for her, the feelings became stronger and more real, and again I was enveloped in liquid heat.

For the next few days I continued to feel compelled to pray for her. Then, I heard a whisper. It seemed to come from the inner depth of my soul but at the same time filled the room: "Call Noreen."

At first I thought my imagination was playing tricks on me. I kept praying in my heavenly language, trying to ignore it, but I couldn't. The more I prayed, the louder it became, and the more I felt it tugging at my heart. *This can't be!* I thought.

I waited. I couldn't summon the courage to call. Two weeks passed, but the tug on my heart was relentless. I rehearsed my excuses: *What could I possibly say to her?*

One morning as I wrestled with this assignment, the Lord answered, "I will give you the words. Trust Me."

Another month passed. Again in prayer, I felt myself overcome by God's presence. I could no longer resist. I picked up the phone and dialed, my hand shaking. I was so nervous, I wanted to hang up before she came on the line, but she answered. I didn't identify myself. I simply shared some things that were on my heart. She listened and thanked me. I was about to hang up when she said, "Wait! Do you know how I can get hold of a woman named Belma?"

I stiffened. "Why?"

"Because I have to tell her I'm so sorry!"

My heart melted and tears rolled down my face. The Lord's presence intensified. His anointing flowed through the telephone wires. I identified myself, and the conversation that followed lasted three and a half hours. My ex-husband had left her too.

The next day Noreen and I spoke another three hours. We called each other for two weeks, almost every day. God gave me love and compassion for this woman. She was alone with her children, struggling to make ends meet. I was able to share my faith with her—another miracle.

Four weeks went by, and though I stopped calling, I kept praying for Noreen on a daily basis. Again I felt a tug on my heart. During one of my prayer times, I saw what the Lord wanted me to do.

In my spirit He gave me a picture of my car filled with groceries, clothes and toys for Noreen and her children, so I went shopping. It took six weeks to get everything.

When I had prayed over every item, I called Noreen. We met on a Sunday morning, close to my church. A blast of secular music issued from her car when she opened the door. She stepped out, looking slightly confused. A Rottweiler and a baby who resembled my ex-husband waited inside.

I noticed that Noreen looked as nervous as I felt. It was an awkward meeting. I prayed silently in the Spirit for God's strength. Suddenly the comforting heat rose in me again and I sensed His presence. From that moment I felt peace and knew our time together would be blessed. We were in the centre of His perfect will.

I opened my car doors to reveal the food, toys and other provisions and asked her to open her trunk so I could load the things into her car.

ANOTHER WORLD

Noreen stared in disbelief, eyes wide and mouth open. "What are you doing?" she sputtered.

"This is for you." I filled her car with groceries: canned goods, treats for the kids, veggies, fruit, cereal boxes—everything imaginable. She sobered as she calculated the dollar value of the goods finding their way into her trunk. "I'm going to have to pay you back for all of this."

"No, I don't want you to pay it back," I assured her. "Just receive it as a gift." I kept loading until the trunk was full. She took the dog out of the back seat, and I almost filled that too. There was hardly any room for him after I had transferred everything. The car was packed, and we couldn't squeeze in another item.

The Holy Spirit's presence became so strong that Noreen couldn't stand her secular music. "Wait," she said. "I have to turn this off. It's driving me crazy." Then she started to cry. "No one has ever done anything like this for me before. Why are you doing it?"

"It's in my heart to do it." I smiled.

"But what will I tell my children?"

"Just tell them God loves them." I gave her one of my children's videos that contains the salvation message. I knew they would enjoy it, and I hoped they could receive Jesus through it.

Noreen, still shocked, shook her head. "I feel like I'm in another world." I smiled. Momentarily we were.

We talked for an hour, immersed in God's love. After we said goodbye, with an open heart she gave me a long hug, got in her car and left.

As I drove away, I was at peace. I knew God had His hand on Noreen and her children. A desire to intercede for them came over me, and I wept for their salvation. Again heat from that "other world" filled my car, and in my spirit I saw Noreen, her children and myself standing in the throne room before God, our Father. Jesus was standing behind us, His arms on our shoulders. It looked like there were wings of protection hovering over the children. A sweet whisper filled my car: "Those children do not belong to you, Belma, and they do not belong to Noreen. They belong to Me. Whatsoever you have done to them, you have done to Me."

The curtain of Heaven closed, and the vision was gone. I felt that God was pleased.

I am humbled that through Noreen God gave me the opportunity to live His Word. Jesus says, "And I, if I be lifted up from the earth, will draw all men unto me" (John 12:32, KJV). When I allowed Jesus to flow into the lives of Noreen and her children, He was exalted and had the opportunity to draw them to Himself.

WALLS

A few minutes later when I walked into my church I was still deep in the spirit realm. People were in praise and worship, but as I looked around I clearly saw who was entering into God's presence and who was just there in body, going through motions. I wondered why they were in church at all. It made me sad for them and for Jesus.

There is no end to how much praise we can offer God for His faithfulness toward us. We all have many things for which to praise Him. He healed and restored my broken heart. He washed away my grief, hopelessness, despair, anger and bitterness and replaced them with His unconditional love and peace. I can't stop thanking Him.

I know now that when we harbour anger and bitterness we destroy ourselves. We put up walls that keep us from receiving from God. These walls collapse as we pray and obey God to carry out the desires of His heart. After they fall, we hear God more clearly. Now in my prayer times He makes Himself very real to me and shows me His thoughts and ways.

GOD INCIDENTS

My experience with Noreen is one of many God-ordained encounters that happened to me while serving on the ministry prayer team at the Catch the Fire Church. During those 20 years tremendous love and compassion have grown in my heart for God's people. I see how hungry they are for God and how broken the world is. I am humbled that God uses me to pray for people from nations all over the globe. They stand in prayer lines, their faces upward, hands outstretched, longing for a touch from Almighty God, and I ache to see them healed and whole. What an honour to witness God's power, love, grace and mercy poured out on them.

I remember a woman who was really nervous when I asked if I could pray for her. She had never been "slain in the Spirit" and absolutely did not want to fall on the floor. I assured her that she did not have to be on the ground to receive what God had for her. She could receive standing right where she was.

She seemed relieved. "Good," she said, "because I want to stand all the way through it."

I was standing about 18 inches from her, not touching her. I had barely prayed one sentence when she screamed and toppled. She lay on the floor, not twitching a muscle.

I prayed over her for a while and moved on. Later I went back to see how she was doing. She told me a tremendous power hit her, unlike anything she'd ever known. As she lay there, the Lord gave her a "hospital" experience, as if on an "operating table." She and others on the carpet underwent spiritual surgery.

She now saw the ministry team as "doctors" and "nurses" through whom the chief physician, Jesus, was laying His healing hands on everyone. I was astonished at the apt comparison.

It's always a privilege to hear what God is doing in people's hearts. I'm excited and blessed to watch others get blessed. It makes me want to pray more.

One of the greatest outcomes of the revival at Catch the Fire was the gathering of every limb of the body of Christ in one place for one purpose. Many churches from every denomination came together in unity to worship before Him. We loved and served each another. It reminds me of the Scripture "that their hearts might be comforted, being knit together in love" (Colossians 2:2, KJV).

During this time of spiritual revival the next step in my journey unfolded.

Chapter 12

Forgiveness and Honour

Honor your father and mother...that it may go well with you.

EPHESIANS 6:2–3, ESV

Eight months after my grandfather's death, I received a phone call from a lawyer in Berlin. By now my mother had been in Germany for 17 months. He said, "We have your mother in custody. Your grandparents left you a copy of a will, and she has stolen your inheritance. This action will put her in prison for life."

"I have a copy of the will here, and I'm supposed to get half," I replied.

"That's right," he responded, "but she has taken your name off and put her name in, stealing your half. However, she's been caught. We need you to come to Germany so we can see you in person to verify your existence, and then we can put her in jail. That's the law of this country."

I was stunned. The information was more than I could handle. Too many difficult things were happening in my life at the time. "I can't talk about it right now. You'll have to call me back tomorrow," I told him.

Just then God intervened. I saw a vision of an old woman. It was my mother. She was sitting on cement, getting older in a jail cell. An unexpected thought crossed my mind. *Jesus wouldn't do that to His mother. Why would I do it to my mother?*

The lawyer I had spoken to was a Christian whom I had met several times. He phoned back the next day, but I was still sorting it out in my mind. "If I come to Germany, you'll put her in jail right away. If I don't come, you won't. Is that correct?"

The lawyer agreed but reminded me, "The Bible says, 'Give to Caesar what belongs to Caesar.' You have a right to your inheritance, and you need to come here and claim it. That's biblical."

"But I can't put my mother in jail for money."

"She'll get her portion and yours if you don't come," he warned. It was a sizable sum—about half a million dollars, rather than the quarter million we each should have received. "If you come here, you will receive *all* of it."

For two weeks the lawyers in Berlin and Toronto tried to persuade me to go to Germany. I just couldn't do it. "I'm sorry; I can't," I apologized. "You can let my mother go. I forgive her. It's okay."

Sometimes things happen in life beyond our understanding. Though my mother wasn't jailed, because of her crime she was legally banished from Germany for life. She took the whole $500,000 and with my portion bought a yacht. It was shipped from the United States to Canada. She and Helmut enjoyed it for a few years. One day, long after the fact, I heard that during one of their boating excursions there was a boating accident. Helmut had fallen overboard and drowned. After that my mother sold the yacht and put herself into a jail of her own making.

A SELF-MADE JAIL

She became a recluse. For almost 19 years she imprisoned herself in her own home. I had no more contact with her. After her death neighbours told me the only way she communicated was by notes through the mail slot. "Cut my grass. Here's the money," a note would say. She snuck out at night to buy groceries, opened her garage door with a remote, backed out in the dark, and came home unseen. She made purchases by catalogue or phone, became a hoarder, and clung to everything from the time she came to Canada in 1952.

During my years of alienation from my mother, God fast-tracked His purpose for my life. I received a bachelor of arts degree from my accumulated college points, and thinking I wanted to be a doctor, I applied to and was accepted into medical school. But God had another plan. I found myself at a crossroads between ministry and medicine. The Lord said I could choose either, and He would bless it, but if I chose ministry, there would be a high cost and sacrifice. "I will never leave you or forsake you," He promised. I chose ministry.

In January 2009, when my mother was 78 years old, I got a call from her doctor. Despite the fact that she had told him she didn't have any children and had never been married, my name was on her records. The doctor informed me, "Your mother has passed away. Her heart stopped.

We need someone to come and identify her body." My mother had been a very heavy smoker and had finally succumbed to atrial fibrillation.

I drove to the hospital. There she lay, no longer able to hurt me. I gazed at her still body, ran my fingers through her once luxuriant hair and asked the nurse if she would please uncover her. I wanted to see her hands and her feet.

19 YEARS LATER

I had an intense desire to see her. I hadn't seen her for almost 20 years. I looked at her pale face with regret. Her walls had been impenetrable. Her being, untouchable. Now, in death the walls were down. No more could she refuse me. I reached out and touched her hands and feet. I had never been this close to her. It was my last chance at an intimacy no longer hers to forbid.

I sat beside her for a long time, feeling the texture of the skin on her feet, tracing the veins in her hands and recognizing the effects of time, bitterness and pain on her face. As I leaned over her, my face close to hers, a tear spilled from my eye and ran down her cheek.

After making the formal identification, I left my mother's body in storage at the hospital. I had no idea what to do with it. Who would go to her funeral? She didn't know anybody, and nobody knew her.

At the end of the week the hospital pressured me to make funeral arrangements. I asked for her to be moved to a funeral home. When after several days I hadn't firmed up plans, the funeral director began to exert pressure on me to bury her. I decided on cremation. When he asked me what I wanted done with the ashes, again I didn't know, and I asked him to keep them for a while. He just shook his head.

Then began the difficult task of untangling her worldly affairs. I went to my mother's lawyer to start the long, lonely process.

Next was cleaning out her house. It took me seven months to get it ready to sell. I didn't take any ministry bookings during that time.

A HOARDER'S HAVEN

The interior of my mother's house was shocking. I was horrified at the filth and the mountains of clothes, books, magazines, newspapers and many other items she had hoarded, but I wasn't surprised. The house reeked of smoke. Everywhere mounds of dirty laundry covered the furniture. Not a table or chair was visible. The dining room was filled with piles of clothes, many that had never been worn and still had sales tags on them. Everything she had taken from my birth father was there, including marriage certificates, old passports and paperwork.

To make matters worse, she hadn't been able to bend over and pick things up without falling because she had been heavily drugged for severe back pain. It was heart-wrenching to think that she had been sick and unable to care for herself, yet all the while she had a daughter who looked after others and would have loved to help her. But she had chosen to suffer alone. I wept thinking of it. How I had wanted to be a daughter to her!

In all the mess of material things she had accumulated around her, one thing stood out most. I could see my mother's desperation in trying to find solace for her soul in every item she collected. The clothes, the shoes and purses, the jumble of purchases new and unused, and the papers, documents and old photographs in disarray within the walls of her house reflected the condition of her tormented soul.

She had collected many things—things that brought momentary, fleeting comfort. I knew they could never bring her the peace or fulfillment her heart sought, but the fortresses in her mind would not allow anything else in. The world outside her walls was her enemy, and I was part of that world.

I took in her prison. Deep sadness and grief flooded me for her sake. The stillness and silence that hung in the air encroached upon me as if it had personality. It screamed of the thoughts, pains and regrets that had consumed her. What torturous days she must have spent in this claustrophobic cell!

The pounding of my heart dispelled the silence, and as it did, a question gripped me. With every beat and every breath it grew stronger and louder: Where did my mother make her eternal home?

THE NEIGHBOURS

A handyman, the only one she ever allowed into her house, pointed me to a chair in the living room—her favourite place. She sat there day in, day out, smoking, he said. The last time I saw her, at my grandfather's deathbed, she had screamed that she wanted nothing to do with me, but she died surrounded by magazines, magazine covers, newspaper spreads and images of me modelling. Was it a sign?

When she looked at those pictures, did the Lord remind her of the time she prayed the sinner's prayer with me? That was the only time she had ever allowed me into her world. When we prayed, I saw the connection. Tears, like rare jewels, spilled from her eyes. The light of God penetrated her darkness ever so briefly to give her a glimpse of a reality beyond her own. For just that one moment she could see clearly, and I could see deep into her soul.

One thing that surprised and delighted me was to see a Billy Graham book called *The Way* in her possession. It renewed my hope that our conversation and prayer had touched her. *Why else would she have kept it?* I reasoned.

Before long I met all the neighbours. "You're her daughter?" They were incredulous. "We are so happy to meet you. We tried to help your mother. We tried to talk to her, but after your stepfather died she never once talked to us."

When I started to clean out the house, I invited them to visit anytime. They brought food and, if I had to stay over, gave me blankets and helped in many ways. Rudi, a 78-year-old man, came by. He listened to me and my Christian friends chat as we painted the walls, and he said, "You people talk like my neighbour." His neighbour was a Christian, and one day, at the end of my mother's driveway, Rudi committed his life to the Lord.

A PAINFUL REVELATION

To clean out my mother's house was a difficult task. I found an abundance of troubling evidence pertaining to her theft of my inheritance, and I learned many things. After gaining access to my money, she went to the bank to withdraw $1,000 bills. All the receipts were there. I found where she tried to change the will and saw how she practiced writing my grandparent's signature. That turned my stomach.

Then I found Oma's diary. She had written about my mother abusing her and how she lost the heart to live. She worried about my mother interrogating her and putting pressure on her to sign papers she didn't want to sign. She wrote, "I can't fight her anymore. I can't live like this. I don't want to live anymore. It's too painful. I just can't go on." It broke my heart. I could hardly read it.

A year and a half later when I started to work things through with my counsellor, Lorne Shepherd, I was done in and overwhelmed by the magnitude of issues surrounding my mother: the paperwork, finding Oma's diary, and learning what she had done to my dad. She was a criminal. I was floundering at the abundance of unwelcome revelations, but her doctor told me she had a mental disorder. That put things into better perspective.

Under Lorne's direction I came to see my mother with new eyes. He guided me to think of her as a wounded child. The Lord gently reminded me that she had brought me into this world and that she belonged to my beloved Oma.

Then I remembered an open vision I had received shortly after accepting the Lord. It was about my life prior to conception and even before I was in my mother's womb. In the vision I lived in spirit form in Heaven with the Father. It was as though I was a child, but I didn't have a body as we know it. I was a spirit and at home with my Father. It was different from being a child on earth.

HONOURING GOD'S CHOICE

I remember being very bendable and flexible, and my Father was delighted with me. I was fully accepted, loved, fulfilled and free. I fit in every way. I lacked nothing. His presence filled me and the atmosphere around me. We were one. There was total trust, transparency and openness between us with nothing hidden. Pure love, but yet we were individuals. I belonged to Him and I was safe, surrounded by peace and joy. I sensed the presence of other spirit children in the background, but my Father's focus was on me. I was the most important thing on His mind at that moment.

"I have to send you down there," I heard my Father say. "I have a plan for you to fulfill on earth. I need you to carry it out."

I didn't want to go, but He said, "I need you to go. Don't worry. I Myself will take you." He pulled me into His arms, close to His being, and suddenly, with a swishhhh, down we went to earth. We seemed to fly at the speed of light. The next moment I was in my mother's womb.

I still wonder if that might have been the instant when my human father's sperm fertilized my mother's egg and God ignited the union with life. He says we are "eternal beings" and that means we have always existed in some form and will always exist: He was there… (see Psalm 139: 13–16).

As pieces of the picture came together under Lorne's guidance, I realized that my heavenly Father could have chosen any womb, but He chose Ingeborg's, and I had to honour His choice.

This understanding changed me. I now looked at family albums and thought, *Wow! If it weren't for Ingeborg, I wouldn't be here and I wouldn't be serving the Lord.*

A year and a half after my mother's death I was healed sufficiently to want to honour her. In the course of those 18 months I had received an injection of supernatural love for her that softened my heart. *What can I do to honour her?* I wondered. I started planning her funeral.

I called my pastor friend Mary Audrey Raycroft and asked if she could perform a funeral service. She planned for it as though 10,000 people were attending, when in fact I would probably be the only one there. It was a rainy September. It rained every day except for the one I chose for the funeral. That day the birds sang and the sun shone brightly. We held it outside, and Mary Audrey looked after the details. I invited a dear friend who is a photographer to take pictures so I would have memories of this very special occasion.

We picked a song by one of my mother's favourite artists, Andre Rieu, "The Angels Are Dancing." In my mind I saw them dancing with joy because my mom was being buried with honour.

I bought six roses, representing myself, Opa, Oma, God the Father, the Son and the Holy Spirit. I made them into a beautiful bouquet. The funeral was as formal as it would have been for a full house.

"We would like to begin with Ingeborg's favourite song," Mary Audrey announced, and she blasted "The Angels Are Dancing" on the CD player. I smiled. The funeral director and 10,000 angels stood by watching.

When the funeral director brought me the ashes, I hugged them to my chest. A wave of heat surged through me—a hug from my mom, I imagined.

The ashes were in a very pretty container. I lowered it and the roses into the ground. It was a good memorial service and meant much to me. I am so grateful to Mary Audrey for her sensitivity and for taking time and care to make it special. I was content. My mom was honoured, and the Lord was pleased. It was the best funeral I had attended.

After the funeral I had a dream that I was in Heaven. A choir was singing, and I felt a hand on my shoulder. It was Jesus. He walked me into a room where my mother stood. I put my arms around her. She hugged me from her heart. It was a profound one-on-one connection. In the dream I thought, *That's what a mother's hug feels like.* It was so comforting. She held me a long time, and I drank it in. I awoke, but I could still feel the hug.

I felt the hug for three weeks in the natural realm as if my mother was still there. It was so real and life-giving!

Since that dream I have no doubt my mother is in Heaven. I am so glad I followed the Lord's prompting and didn't put her in jail. "Vengeance is mine...says the Lord" (Romans 12:19, ESV). In other words, I didn't have to punish my mother for what she did. God knew better what the situation required.

The truth is, I didn't lose my inheritance to my mother. To walk pleasing to the Lord and be in His perfect will turns out better for us than anything we might want to do. I gained an inheritance in my Father God, and that's so much more important to me than money. God forgave her, and so did I. I have peace, my conscience is clear, and the windows of Heaven opened to pour out a blessing for me to walk in the destiny He had prepared (see Malachi 3:10).

Pause and Reflect

We were in God's plans before creation; God knew us before we were born! Belma's experience speaks to those who feel they are an "accident," that they should not have been born, or that their life has no purpose.

Have you ever been tempted to rue the day you were born like Job (see Job 3:1) or Jeremiah (see Jeremiah 20:14)?

Explain what you were going through to provoke such thoughts. Can you find comfort in knowing that Bible heroes had similar reactions?

How does it make you feel to know that somehow He saw you before any of the creation had even been brought forth?

I believe that Belma's mother transferred the pain she endured as a child onto Belma. When she rejected her daughter, she was rejecting the little girl who had been abused. She wanted to detach herself from the shame of that little girl. Her way of doing it was to detach herself from Belma.

When someone has experienced significant wounding, that person may sometimes deal with a demonic influence behind it. Ingeborg transferred her pain to Belma because she had never resolved it within herself.

Has it ever occurred to you that someone's rejection of you could actually be a rejection of their own self?

What do you think it means to transfer pain to somebody else?

Is there a better way to deal with unresolved issues?

Identify any unresolved issues in your own life, and make a plan for how you will deal with them.

Chapter 13

Preparation

And they went forth...everywhere, the Lord working with them,
and confirming the word with signs following.

MARK 16:20, KJV

In 1991 I attended an International Christian Dance Fellowship conference in Philadelphia. It was organized by Valerie Henry. Valerie was the soloist and main choreographer for the Christian Celebration during the Feast of Tabernacles from 1984 to 2000 in Jerusalem, Israel. I had met her at a Toronto church where she was holding a dance workshop, and subsequently I trained under her many times.

The International Christian Dance Fellowship is a wonderful association that connects dancers from all over the world. Some years after this conference I was appointed national coordinator of the Christian Dance Fellowship of Canada.

At that same conference I attended a workshop called "Dance from the Heart" with instructor Karen Christian from France. It intrigued me because my worship dance is "from the heart." In the workshop I stayed at the back to be alone with the Lord.

"You! At the back!" The instructor's command shook me from my quiet contemplation. Her finger was pointing directly at me. "I want to meet with you at the end of the class."

I was deep in intimacy with the Lord for the remainder of the class, and it affected me profoundly. By the end of the workshop I was undone. When Karen came to speak to me, I could hardly move. I wanted to keep basking in the Lord's presence.

Karen spoke with confidence and authority. "The Lord told me you are to come to France and I am to train you—for free. You just need to get over there. I will impart everything I have into you."

What an honour! I felt like I had just been handed a scholarship. It was amazing, thrilling and humbling at the same time. But very quickly reality sobered me, and the great honour seemed to retreat out of reach.

"Karen, that's a wonderful opportunity," I said. "There's nothing I would like more than to accept your invitation, but I can't. My husband just left me, and I don't have any money."

Karen wasn't swayed. "I know what the Lord said," she insisted. "We're going to pray."

The next month Karen called from France and asked if I had thought any more about coming. She offered me accommodations at a friend's house in nearby Avignon, saying I could house-sit for a month and have the entire house to myself. It sounded so delightful and appealing. Again she reiterated that I only need pay for the flight.

Amazing Provision

I told Karen the flight would cost $864.63. Just then the doorbell rang. I asked her to wait a moment while I responded. It was the postman with a registered letter. I went back to the phone, ripped open the envelope and pulled out my income tax refund. I could hardly believe what I saw! It was a Canadian cheque for $864.63!

I was awestruck! Karen was excited and delighted and couldn't wait for me to come. What amazing provision by God, and what a confirmation that I should go! As we rejoiced, Karen encouraged me to book my flight right away. There was one seat left, and I booked it.

Six weeks later I landed in France. Karen was unable to meet me but sent her girlfriend, who had a little Volkswagen convertible. What a treat! With our hair flying and my suitcases piled in the back, we drove along winding little roads through the picturesque countryside, stopping here and there for sheep crossings. It was a little piece of Heaven. I couldn't stop marvelling at God's goodness.

By the time we arrived in Avignon, I was exhausted. I fell into bed and went to sleep. During the night I awoke to see a large image of the devil on the wall right in front of me. *Oh! It's you again*, I thought and I fell back to sleep. God was with me. I had no worries. When I had arrived I hadn't noticed the poster because of my exhaustion. It was part of the room's décor.

MENTORED

Karen took me under her wing and mentored me for a month. She taught me so much more than worship dance. She was very sensitive to the Holy Spirit and walked a highway of holiness. It was beautiful to see her faith and wisdom. We strolled down the street during Mardi Gras in France, and when the revellers came toward us, she said, "Don't look any of them in the eye; just keep your head down." It reminded me of going to school after the wall went up. Oma would say, "Don't look up. Don't look any of the Russians in the eye. Just keep your head down."

Karen was best friends with a Christian couple who owned a dance studio in Avignon. One of their passions was prayer, but they were also considered the best teachers in all of France. Along with Karen, they taught me at their studio.

The husband taught the "mock method." If I was doing something incorrectly, he stood in front of me and imitated my wrong actions using sound effects. It was unnerving and unpleasant. I soon realized that I had to perform with perfection or I would be mocked. He was a hard task master. I was so pleased when one day I walked past him and he said, "Très bon! Very good!" The training I received with these three teachers was the best of the best.

A NEW ASSIGNMENT

By 1993 the Lord was opening new doors for me. I had recorded a music CD, and I had a dream that the Lord wanted me to do a "worship dance" video. In the dream He told me if I made a video it would go throughout the world to places I couldn't reach. Then I had a second dream of what the video should contain. Three weeks after the second dream, I had a conversation with God.

"Lord, what are You doing about the video?"

"When are you starting the video?" I heard Him respond.

I was bewildered. "I thought You were doing it."

"No, you are." I think He smiled.

I was scared. I'd never done anything like this in my life. I didn't know how to begin or what to do.

I went in the bathroom and looked in the mirror. Instead of seeing my reflection, I saw a vision—40 eight-by-ten sheets of paper. Each paper had a number from 1 to 40. God peeled back each sheet one by one, starting with number 1. Under each paper I saw a child's face. I recognized the faces of children from a Pentecostal church in Toronto where I had taught several times. I wondered what I was supposed to do with the faces, numbers and papers.

"Go there," the Lord said. "They are ready for you. Call the pastor and meet with him."

"They won't want to do this," I argued. "I was just there. They only do dance for Easter and Christmas specials. They don't have dance in that church," as if He didn't know.

"They are ready for you," He repeated.

The next day when I got enough nerve, I phoned the church. A woman called back in 20 minutes to say the pastor would meet with me on Friday. Friday morning I was there waiting for him. The door opened, and in came the senior pastor, doing a little pirouette. "Belma, whatever you want, we are on board. Use our church, our secretary—whatever you need." I was dumbfounded.

I drove out of the parking lot, turned right and pulled up to a stoplight. When I stopped I saw another vision. More kids. They were dancing. I recognized the people from another church in a nearby town. I knew I was to call them. Emboldened by the evidence of God's faithfulness at the previous church, I called. The pastor said, "We want you to come on Sunday morning and speak about your project."

"Really?" I was surprised. It was a Reformed church. Historically in some Reformed churches worship dance had been as foreign as a visitor from Mars.

"I've never spoken in a church," I said. "I just teach dance."

"We really want you to speak. After we hear your presentation, our elders will meet and decide whether we're on board with you."

I did it. I told them about the video God showed me to make. After the service I waited while the pastor and the elders met. When they emerged, the pastor said, "You did that so well. You said you would finance it yourself. We're on board because you didn't ask for money. You can use our kids as you need."

God seemed to like showing me visions in parking lots. As I drove out of their parking lot I had another one. This time I saw a Mennonite church in a nearby city. The pattern repeated over and over until I had visited seven churches representing seven denominations and a total of 77 children. It was remarkable, because in those days denominations seldom interacted.

Within nine months I was ready to birth my first video production. But I had a problem. I was almost penniless.

HE DOES IT AGAIN

I let God know. "I don't have any money left. I need another $7,862.35 to finish the video."

Where in the world would the money come from? On my way to the mailbox I reasoned with God. "I'll sell my bedroom set, my dining room set, my living room set. I can live out of boxes. I'll get one of those blow-up mattresses." I pulled out an envelope from the government and opened it. It was my income tax refund, for exactly $7,862.35!

He did it again!

Flabbergasted, I fell to my knees right there. I breathed the words, "Thank You, Jesus, for the government!"

With every video I produced I saw the same miraculous supernatural provision of God. I did 14 productions, and each cost anywhere from $25,000 to $58,000. I simply depended on the Lord, and He brought in the money.

In hindsight I see how my seasons in life have been ordered by the Lord. Scripture says that He provides, guides our steps and gives promotion.

I experienced another step forward in 1994 when the International Christian Dance Fellowship (ICDF) conference was held in York, England. The founder of the ICDF, Mary Jones, approached me about becoming the coordinator for the ICDF Network for Children's Dance. It would require me to oversee and network children's dance ministries all over the world. It was a great honour but also a huge responsibility, and it made me nervous. Despite my nervousness, I knew it was an assignment from God, and having no idea what was ahead of me, I accepted.

I was about to be propelled into the nations.

Chapter 14

Into All the World

"Look at the nations and watch—and be utterly amazed.
For I am going to do something in your days that you
would not believe, even if you were told."

HABAKKUK 1:5, NIV

After I returned from France I sat with my pastor and shared what I'd learned. Originally we didn't have dance in our church; however, my pastor took notes, and each Sunday morning he shared a bit with the congregation. He didn't call it "dance." He called it "worship." The congregation grew curious and eventually became hungry for this unique "worship."

One day after a congregational meeting when I was the only one in the sanctuary, I had a vision of the elders and the pastor holding red flags and surrounding the perimeter of the sanctuary. Suddenly something like a huge drop of oil formed in the heavenlies, fell, and covered the men. For some reason the vision really unsettled me. God was up to something again! I ran from the building and drove away. I tried to shake the picture from my mind, but for two nights I couldn't sleep. The Holy Spirit nagged me to tell the pastor. I didn't want to. I was determined not to say anything because it sounded so flaky. I didn't think anyone had to know, but the Lord wouldn't let me forget. Finally, out of frustration, I gave in.

I phoned the pastor and rattled off my message, hoping to get off the phone fast.

"I was at the congregational meeting and saw a vision. I saw the elders doing a presentation waving flags. It sounds kind of stupid and probably will never happen for at least five or six years, but I have to share it with you because I can't sleep."

There was dead air on the other end for too long. A hot flush of embarrassment rose in me. "Uh...I should go. That's all I have to say," I managed.

"Belma, wait." There was urgency in his voice. "Before we hang up, I need to tell you something. I had a meeting with the elders because I believe we are to be involved with you. We thought we were to do something with flags, but we prayed that if it was God's will, He would confirm it by having you call and suggest we do it."

"You're kidding!" I was astounded.

"Not at all," he said. "Can you teach the elders at the next meeting?"

It was a Thursday. The next elders' meeting would be Tuesday—four days away. I would have very little time to prepare. Not only that, but "What am I going to teach them?" I blurted with some anxiety. "I've never taught elders before."

My pastor wasn't at all concerned. "The Lord will show you," he said. "He's in it."

TEACHING ELDERS

I spent the next several days praying and asking the Lord what I was supposed to teach. He directed me to the library. I pulled some history books and learned that flag bearers were very important to battle strategy. Wind on the flags showed warriors from which direction arrows would come. Flags also indicated the location of enemy lines. During battle the bodies of fallen soldiers were piled by the flagpole.

I also read that ships had 36 flag colours, each with a different meaning. When they passed each other, they waved a certain colour to communicate a particular message.

Even with all the preparation, I felt inadequate to teach them. I was shaking when I walked into the elders' meeting, but it went well. As I shared about the flags on ships, one older man jumped up and said he had been a sailor for 40 years. He asked for a purple flag. *Goodness!* I thought. *He knows what a purple flag means!*

When I spoke about the bodies around the flag, another man jumped up, wiping tears. He had been in the Second World War. "I'm in," he said. "I'll take a red flag."

After my talk, the pastor suggested we go upstairs to practice. I organized the men into two lines. It was humorous to see each line trying to be "better" than the other. They had no idea how to hold a flag. Neither did they know what they were doing. I coached them slowly.

We practiced eight weeks for our presentation. The second week when we got together to pray, one of the elders became frustrated with a relationship issue and walked out. Our pastor remained steadfast. He was certain we were to proceed, and he instructed the others to let the man go. We continued practicing.

The day of our presentation arrived. I counted the flags—one per elder—and was putting them in the car to take to church when I heard God say, "You forgot one flag."

"No, Lord," I argued. "Remember? One elder walked out."

I kept getting ready.

"You forgot a flag."

"I did *not*! He's not *in it*," I insisted. God sure was persistent.

I got on the road.

"*You forgot a flag!*" His voice boomed! Startled, I gripped the steering wheel, took the nearest exit and turned around. By the time I reached home I was really annoyed. I grabbed the flag and threw it in the back seat. "There! It's in," I huffed.

When I drove into the church parking lot, the elder who had said he wouldn't participate was waiting. He ran to my car, his face tense with distress. It was like seeing a little boy running toward me. "Belma, last night I repented," he said. "I asked the elders and pastor to forgive me. I want to be in the dance. Can I please be in it?"

He can't possibly be in the dance. He hasn't attended any rehearsals. He has no idea what to do, I thought. "Of course you can! No problem!" I replied.

What had I just said? I stared at him, thinking, *What in the world am I going to do? He doesn't know a thing!*

I was already late because of my disobedience. There was no time to practice. The others were ready to start, and then I got an idea. "We're changing things," I announced. Half the elders would be in the front and half in the back. This format allowed the men to surround the whole interior of the church. I told the elder in question, "You'll be at the back. Just watch what the others do and follow them. When they march, you march."

The elders surrounded the church, whipping their flags. The result was dramatic, and God showed up. A woman who had been on heavy medication for depression for ten years was delivered.

Afterward, our pastor took the pulpit. "I want you to know that we support Belma's ministry. We don't just say it with our mouths, but we do it with our bodies. That's why you saw the demonstration today. You will be seeing a lot more of it. Get ready!"

That is how dance came to our church. The people received this new type of worship and wanted more. The elders asked me to teach festival dance, folk dance, Jewish dance—whatever I could. Every Sunday before church we had an hour of dance class. I did men's, women's and children's workshops. My church became my training ground for international ministry. It wasn't long in coming.

When the Toronto revival began in 1994, I spent a lot of time at nightly meetings and got to know the leadership. While I was on the prayer ministry team, John Arnott, the senior pastor, asked me to pray with a large group of German leaders. One asked me to go to Germany to minister to his congregation, but I declined. I explained that I would never go to Germany again because both my grandparents were gone and I had too many painful memories associated with it.

A year later the German pastor approached me again during a conference at TACF (now CTF, Catch the Fire) and repeated his invitation. In the meantime his son, Andreas, had become a TACF volunteer. One day he gave me a German Scripture calendar from his mother. I hadn't read German for many years, also because of the pain, but I received it graciously.

Another day Andreas came along and handed me chocolates. "My mother sends these for you." He grinned.

The next time CTF held a pastors' meeting, someone came to me and said, "The pastor from Germany wants to meet with you." I was frustrated with his persistence, but because of the family's graciousness, I sought him out. When I sat down beside him, he got on his knees and begged, "Please come to Germany!"

"I'll go," I said, with tears in my eyes.

The pastor and his family were thrilled and paid my expenses. "You will have a safe place," they assured me, and they invited me to stay in their home. "We will do everything we can to make you comfortable."

My trip to Germany was wonderful. There was no pain! I've been back nine times since. On that first occasion, I shared my story. A testimony is very unusual for German people to hear because they don't speak of "private matters" in public, yet by that time I felt free to share everything, because God had healed me.

When I had almost finished speaking, a woman at the back screamed. My story had given her flashbacks to the time when Russian soldiers had killed her husband. "I hate you! I hate you!" she yelled, remembering them. People tried to calm her, but because she had dared to expose her pain, we could minister to her, and the Lord delivered her from hatred.

People became more open. Even the staunch ones unfolded their arms and warmed up. By the end of my first two-week trip, they were dancing with flags. It was wonderful to see God dissolve walls of fear and hatred and set them free.

Shortly after I returned, I got a distraught call from the German pastor. "I need help! People are running around the church with flags, and I don't know what to do with them!" He asked me to go back and teach about flags.

During one visit to Germany, in 1996, a pastor from Lyon, France, called and asked to spend two hours with me. He flew in and took a taxi to the church, and we had lunch. We became acquainted, and he invited me to Austria and France to teach workshops. He emphasized that he was looking for not technical expertise but dance from the heart. He wanted me to teach therapy movement and dance with healing. I agreed to go. He took a picture of me for advertising flyers and returned to France.

That year I flew to France and for two weeks, with the help of an interpreter, conducted the workshops. In a workshop focused on intimacy with Jesus, a woman started running around the gym. I didn't stop her, because by now I recognized when God was doing something. I kept teaching and let her run. At the end of two weeks the woman shared her story.

LIVING BRANCHES

As a young girl she had been sexually abused every day by her father. Afterward she would get dressed, run into the forest and hug a tree. It was her only source of comfort. In the workshop where she was learning intimacy with Jesus, she relived her childhood experience of being raped by her father. She ran around the gym looking for the forest, and unable to find it, she panicked. Then suddenly in a corner she saw a tree and ran to it. When she reached out to hug it, the branches extended toward her and became the arms of Jesus. "My daughter," He said, "If you hug Me by faith today, I will heal you."

By faith she hugged Him, and as she did, a numbness in her physical body left her. Life flooded her soul, and that night, for the first time in 27 years of marriage, she made love to her husband with feeling and emotion. She slept well and hadn't had nightmares since.

What a testimony! I asked the Lord why He hadn't told me earlier her reason for running around the gym. "I want the glory to be Mine," He responded.

A BIG BELLY

We did another workshop on rejection. A large ebony-black African woman with a gigantic midriff was there. During the workshop she dropped to the floor and rolled from one side of the gym to the other—a ball going back and forth, back and forth. Her 17-year-old daughter was flabbergasted at her mother's behaviour—all we could see were the whites of her eyes, wide with surprise, following her mother each way.

That night, at two o'clock in the morning, we were startled awake to jubilant screams from the bathroom. It was the black woman. "What is she doing?" we exclaimed as we jumped out of bed.

We rushed in to see. There she was, in front of the mirror, doing a jig, screaming and singing, "I am a daughter of the King." The massive distension was gone.

"Where is your stomach?" someone gasped.

"The Lord took it!" she shouted. "Wait till my husband sees me!" Her husband had rejected her throughout their marriage because of her grossly distended middle.

We stayed there laughing, looking around, just taking in the wonder.

"Don't look around," she said. "The Lord took my stomach! It's gone. It's flat. See?" She pulled up her large T-shirt to show us. "It's gone!"

The miracle built great faith among everyone who attended the workshop.

SMELL OF SIN

In another workshop in France, a man continually left the room when we were in a time of intimacy with the Lord and came back afterward smelling of smoke. I found it frustrating. "Lord, he's missing it," I complained. "He's leaving at the most important part of the workshop."

At the end of two weeks that man was the first to give his testimony. He spoke French, and the interpreter translated. "I couldn't handle it when we got close to God," he said. "I had to go out for a cigarette. But Jesus sat with me while I smoked. Last night, I gave my heart to Him, and now I'm a Christian."

I was ashamed. "Lord, I repent for thinking there was nothing going on out there when this man was having a smoke. He wasn't missing You at all! I repent for judging." I wiped away tears. Why should God be limited to a workshop? He's omnipresent!

NOT AFRICA!

In my travels, as I teach worship dance, I have had to repent a number of times when God gives me understanding of the circumstances.

I love to travel and teach, but there was one place I never wanted to go. "Don't send me to Africa," I begged the Lord. "I'm afraid to go there, and it's too far away."

One day in 1997 I had an open vision of riding in a jeep. I was in Africa, travelling south, sitting behind Jesus while He was driving. He threw His head back in laughter. *Well, this is interesting! Jesus is driving me to Africa,* I thought.

The next day at church a woman told me that an African pastor was staying at her house. She had shown him one of my videos the previous evening. After seeing the video, the pastor said he needed me to go to Africa.

It wasn't hard to figure out that God had shown me the vision for this purpose. The woman introduced me to Andrew and his wife, Theresa, and they extended an invitation to Africa.

How could I say no to God?

On the plane I was assigned a seat at the back with noisy kids. An irate woman beside me was screaming at the flight attendant because

I was supposedly sitting in her friend's seat. It was actually my seat. Flustered, the flight attendant tried to calm her, but the woman escalated the ruckus until I stood and told the flight attendant to give the seat to her friend. It didn't matter to me where I sat.

The flight attendant was appreciative, but in her busyness, she forgot me and left me standing in the aisle. When the plane's door closed, I sought her out to remind her that I needed a seat. She grabbed my hand, led me to first class, plunked me down in a seat and spread a white tablecloth in front of me. I chuckled, thinking, *Jesus is taking me out for dinner tonight.* It was the best!

On my way to Africa, we had a 12-hour layover in Germany. When I stepped off the plane a surprise met me. A couple waving a big sign, "Welcome Belma Vardy," was there to greet me. What a delight! Some Canadian friends had notified them of my layover and asked them to care for me while I was there. The couple took me to their home, fed me, and told me to make myself comfortable while they were at work. They would be back to make dinner for me and take me to the airport. I was free to take a leisurely bath and sleep all day. It was luxurious!

ON TO AFRICA!

From the moment I landed in Pretoria, I was on a whirlwind schedule. I was to teach workshops under a huge tent. Pastor Andrew had invited me to his church, but the others didn't want to miss out. It intrigued them that I was from "Toronto," where people were "falling in the Spirit" and revival was happening. They wanted the Holy Spirit too, but they didn't want anyone to fall down in their churches. Their leaders came to check me out before they invited me to make sure I wouldn't influence anyone to fall.

SCRUTINIZED

While I was doing a workshop with the youth at Pastor Andrew's church, 17 staunch African church leaders sat in three rows to watch. I was practicing a presentation with the youth, standing on a table at the back, directing them. When we finished, I went forward to lead the youth in a prayer with movement.

As I was praying with my eyes closed, I heard the sound of a rushing wind against the tent. I opened my eyes to see half the youth on the floor. They had fallen under the power of the Spirit.

I gasped, thinking, *The church leaders! What has the Lord done?* Things had been moving along uneventfully until then, and now I was having a screaming conversation in my head with God.

Predictably, the leaders were fuming. They gathered around Pastor Andrew. "You said she wouldn't make them fall, and they're all falling on the ground!" one of them declared with a broad sweep of his arm.

The manifestation of the Holy Spirit among the youth apparently hadn't ended. The leaders noticed that more young people were affected. They rushed to the back to separate those who were still standing from those who had fallen, but to no avail. More youth wobbled on their feet and went down. Not only were they falling, but by now they were starting to manifest the presence of the Holy Spirit. Some were laughing, some rolling, and others were shaking. It was "Toronto" at its grandest.

But I didn't even touch them, I wailed in my thoughts. *They're here to check me out, and this is getting really bad, Lord!* I had done all I knew to do, so I turned to Pastor Andrew and offered meekly, "I think perhaps I will turn the meeting over to you now." I could see the *Thanks, Belma!* in his eyes.

I sat quietly with my back to the leaders. They had been running back and forth throughout the church trying to contain what they couldn't understand and were now huddled in the rows right behind me.

Eventually everyone left, and at eleven o'clock at night, we went home. The phone rang as we walked through the door. One of the leaders wasn't done yet. Still livid, he railed against Pastor Andrew. I was discouraged and felt bad for him that they should pursue him with such fury.

NOT HAPPY

It surprised me that the next morning these same elders still wanted me to teach a workshop on intimacy with God at their church. I was resentful and disappointed with their negative attitude toward me. In hindsight, I was behaving carnally myself. I should have released the situation into God's hands, knowing He had brought me to Africa.

The church was huge—a far cry from Pastor Andrew's tent. It was an evangelical non-charismatic assembly that held four services each Sunday.

I had no interest or enthusiasm to be there. Compelled to do my "job," in the adult workshop I shared my story, thinking, *Nobody will get it.*

In the "Intimacy with Jesus" workshop where all the leaders participated, I wasn't feeling the least bit spiritual. As I was going through the motions, I noticed that the men were wiping tears. *Why are they crying?* I wondered. As the music faded, I asked, "Would somebody like to share what's happening?"

One of the men responded, "The Lord showed me my heart. I'm into pornography, and I shouldn't be." He broke into deep, heaving sobs. I was humbled. I hadn't expected that at all.

God was moving. One by one the men revealed their sins, and I repented. "Let's continue," I said, turning up the music. "We need to go deeper." I leaned against the wall and wept, asking God to forgive me. I was indescribably sorry for prejudging these people and their situation.

SHAKEN

"When you go back to Canada, Belma, I want you to give testimony how I changed your heart, and how I dealt with you," God said. I was so convicted and wept so deeply, mascara began running down my face. I wiped away what I could, stopped the music and looked at the men. They were really grappling with deep issues.

When Pastor Andrew returned to pick me up, I was still emotionally shaken. He saw me with makeup smeared on my face and became alarmed. "What happened to you? What's with those people?" he demanded, thinking I had been under attack again. I quickly explained that I had lacked understanding and been defensive and arrogant and that God had changed my attitude.

The leadership wanted me back again for the afternoon to teach their children and prepare a presentation for the next day's service. Pastor Andrew brought me to the church. Ready to trust God and submit myself to Him, knowing He had a greater plan, I taught the children. The elders sat at the back to "observe," and the children were good.

Nothing questionable happened, but then I became aware of the sound of someone crying in the hallway. I discovered that some of the young people were grieved. They wanted a dance class too. The leaders, trying to protect them from what God did at the other church, didn't want me to teach them. I felt sad and asked God what I could do.

I suggested that we incorporate the young people in a song with the children carrying flags and marching down the aisle. The elders were nervous. They asked to see the song. I performed it with the children, and they approved it for youth participation. We presented at both morning services, and people were blessed and touched.

HEAR AND OBEY

While I was in Africa, on the home front, my assistant, Heather, was making 100 flags for my next trip to Germany. We had planned at some point for her to come with me to help tape a video for the German people. Half was to be filmed in Canada with Canadian youth and half in Germany with German youth. I expected to marry the two groups in the dance video.

I returned from Africa on a Saturday and was to fly out on Tuesday. Heather gave me the flags at church and was radiantly happy. She and her husband, John, invited me to go to lunch with them. I loved the idea. "Okay!" I said.

Just then a voice yelled, "*Noooooo!*" It echoed, as if down a long tunnel that reverberated the words back to me. "Heather, did you hear that?" I asked.

"Hear what?"

I was momentarily puzzled but quickly realized the voice had come from inside me. *It must have been my imagination*, I reasoned, and I asked, "So where are we going?"

"Your favourite chicken chalet!"

No sooner had I said "I love it!" than I heard the voice again. "*Nooooo!*"

We talked for two hours in the parking lot while I wrestled with the inner voice. Finally, I said, "I can't see why I can't go. I'll go."

"*No!*" yelled the voice. "*Don't go!*" This time I knew who was speaking.

I was disgruntled. "I can't go with you. I don't know why, but I can't go. Something inside me is saying no."

I parted from Heather, got in my car and drove home whining. I was upset with God. "Why can't I just go out and enjoy myself with people? I always do ministry," I complained. "I need to get out and have some fun too. I need to eat lunch, You know. I'm hungry!"

I went home in a huff, unpacked my things from Africa and began preparations for my trip to Germany.

The next morning at seven o'clock my phone rang. It was Colleen. "Belma, I've got some bad news. I need to come over."

A flash of alarm burned through me. "Who died?" She wouldn't tell me.

In half an hour she was at my house. "Heather was killed. When they left the church, her son was driving, and her husband was in the front seat. Apparently, they had all fallen asleep. The car hit the curb and flipped six times. Heather wasn't wearing a seatbelt and flew out on the pavement. She died instantly." Grief and shock overwhelmed me. Heather! My good friend and wonderful helper was gone! The joy of our happy reunion in the church parking lot was so fresh in my mind. Had I not obeyed God's voice—that persistent voice that yelled at me—I would have been in the back seat with her and her eight-year-old daughter.

I visited her husband, John, at the hospital. His son was unconscious. He had been pinned under the car. John told me that Heather's funeral would be Thursday and asked if I would stay for it and dance as a memorial to her.

From the funeral I went directly to the airport and flew to Germany. It was a tough flight.

A Fax From Home

In Germany I not only had to train the youth for the video but also had to speak at a church. Again my story was traumatic to some of the listeners. The silence surrounding that event had been almost as impenetrable as the wall itself. My story stirred pains long buried. People screamed and fainted. Ambulances rushed in to carry them out. The memories were just too overwhelming.

On another trip to Germany, as I continued to prepare for the video production, a fax from my church arrived at the house where I was staying. A sense of foreboding seized me. They only sent faxes in a dire emergency.

The news was worse than I expected. James and Alana, the two main Canadian youth dancers from my home church who were to be in the video, were killed in a car accident.

I read the fax, and my arms dropped. Tears poured down my cheeks, and words wouldn't come. The pastor and his wife took me into their arms and held me as I wept for my beloved young people in Canada. Heather, and now these two precious youths from my church.

They had skidded on black ice and had been hit by an oncoming car. This was just six months after Heather's death. Not only was I grieving for these two young people, but what was I to do with the video? The Canadian and German youth had been very excited about interacting with each other and visiting each other's countries. They had been looking forward to becoming friends, but it wasn't to be. The Lord said, "When you get back to Canada, don't make them do it." I knew He meant for me not to involve the Canadian youth in the video. They were too overcome with grief.

I had never encountered the kind of spiritual opposition I did with this video. It was fraught with resistance and took nine months to produce. The enemy tried to stop it, kill it, steal it and destroy it. He found every angle to try to prevent it from being made. I kept going. I knew God wanted me to produce it.

I believed in the project so much that I saved every penny and put it back into this work of God. I even paid the expenses of a television studio's cameraman and producer-director to help me film.

It was now 1999, just months since the tragedy. I arrived with a crew in Germany. It had been raining for six weeks, and our filming was scheduled over a two-week period. What were the chances we would get good weather?

Every day while we practiced, it rained. I encouraged everyone to pretend it wasn't raining so we could accomplish what we needed to start filming.

RAIN OR NO RAIN

It kept raining. After the first week I wondered if we would return home without a film, but that Thursday night I received a call saying it wouldn't rain the next day. I decided to hire the cameras. Once the rental fees were paid, we wouldn't be able to back out. If it rained, I would lose a lot of money. We took the risk and were ready to go.

Our first location was outside a large church. When we started to film, the German police came by and asked to see our permits. I felt intimidated because of memories of the Russians from my childhood, but I explained the situation: Markus, a leader from one of the churches, had the permits. He was on his way. One policeman wasn't satisfied. He was offended by the Christian music we were blasting in the street. Another delay!

The more we tried to hurry, the slower things moved. I was anxious. We had so little time to film at this location before moving to the next one.

Just then a man came along and asked what was going on. He wanted to know why areas were roped off and he couldn't pass by. I tried to explain in German, but he grew agitated. "Look, I'm the mayor of this town, and I need to know what's happening here," he exclaimed. My director tried to calm him down, but she couldn't speak German. We continued with the filming. He watched for a while and left.

When we finished filming I went to city hall to see the policeman who had been irate about the music and the permit. He was still angry, and he yelled at me again. Suddenly from the back of the room a voice boomed. "What are you doing to this lady? How dare you talk to her like that? Don't you know she's doing a good thing for this town?" I turned to see who was speaking. It was the mayor defending me!

GOD-INTERVENTIONS

God-incidents and God-interventions happened continually. Without them, we couldn't have done the filming. Filming was difficult, and I didn't want to face it. Every day I wanted to stay in bed. Every day I needed a miracle, and every day God sent one.

Another miracle was the mayor's contribution of an endorsement for the back jacket of the video. What a change from when we first met him! But God used him. On the back of the video, he said, "This has been a new and convincing display of faith and devotion."

BREAKING DOWN WALLS

We named the video *Breakout*. This production helped bring reconciliation to the hearts of German, Polish, Dutch and French people. For example, when at a gathering I told my story of surviving the Berlin Wall massacre and showed the video, people of several nationalities, without invitation, came forward, weeping and repenting. Since I am of German descent and represent the German people, they asked me to forgive them for hatred.

One song in particular had a powerful impact. The song "No Other Gods" is a redemptive prayer to take back what was lost. We filmed it on roller skates in the same square where Hitler held his rallies. We used the same colour flags Hitler used, but we raised them in honour of our Lord Jesus Christ. We chose this song because there was a time in Hitler's life when he considered himself a god and wanted the German people to bow before him. He demanded that he be called "master," but the words of the song say, "We shall have no other gods; we shall serve no other master but You, Jesus."

A Dutch woman in her 70s commented, "I need to forgive the German people for what they did to us. During the war the soldiers came into our houses, took everything, and left us with nothing. I've had unforgiveness toward Germans all these years. When I saw the innocent youth in this video trying to take back what the devil has stolen, I recognized the bitterness in my heart, and I am so sorry. Will you forgive me?"

The responses astonished me. God used the arts to bring people to repentance.

God wants to redeem what the evil one has stolen. The video is symbolic of this truth. It begins with the doors of a church opening slowly. The camera pans a wall that symbolizes the Berlin Wall but is actually the wall of the church.

In contrast to the terrified screams of people running through the streets as the Berlin Wall was erected to imprison them, the video celebrates the youth of Germany "breaking out" through open church doors into freedom. This time, waving high the banner of our Lord Jesus, they dance down the streets to spread the good news of the gospel. For God's glory they "break out" into praise and worship in the streets, symbolizing and celebrating freedom in the lives of the German people.

The sound of marching in the streets is no longer that of Hitler's army. It's now the sound of the Army of God.

The audio of flags whipping in praise has been turned up in symbolic contrast to the violent whipping of the people in the streets during World War II.

Cries that came from concentration camps have been replaced by shouts of joy in the Holy Spirit, whose power deposits renewal and healing in people's hearts and throughout the land.

We premiered *Breakout* in Weinstadt, Germany, in a huge church. The response was overwhelming—freedom, tears and healing flowed freely.

If it hadn't been for God's grace to help me move forward, God's will for setting people free through the video would not have been accomplished. As believers, our life's purpose is to yield to God and work with Him for the advancement of His kingdom.

EXUBERANT PRAISE

My source of transformation has been worship. I have learned that in difficult situations we need to worship God and let Him take over. We don't have to deal with circumstances ourselves. We can give them to Him in worship and let Him fight our battles for us. In worship I yield my heart to the Lord, and God breaks down strongholds in me. Strongholds are wrong beliefs and attitudes that prevent us from receiving God's best. When God removes them, we experience new freedom and joy.

Our Heavenly Father is a liberating God!

The familiar words of the doxology sung in many churches express my heart:

Praise God, from whom all blessings flow;
Praise Him, all creatures here below;
Praise Him above, ye heavenly hosts;
Praise Father, Son and Holy Ghost.

I praise Him today for the flow of blessings that come from my heavenly Father's heart to me. I am His precious daughter. In Him alone do I consider myself a blessed woman!

Pause and Reflect

Sometimes God puts us in "boot camp." These are times of preparation when we need to be strengthened in the Spirit. Just like soldiers are trained to obey without questioning, so God trains us. Jesus says we have to "take up [our] cross" (Matthew 16:24; Mark 8:34, NLT) and fight the good fight of faith.

How are you doing in your own obedience training with the Lord?

What do you think it means to pick up your cross and follow Jesus?

Often while we are in training we complain and agonize about how it hurts, but as long as we keep saying "Thy will be done," we move ahead. When we follow Jesus, we walk in victory.

Can you name some victories you've achieved after praying "Thy will be done"?

Praise and worship are our most important weapons in this battle. We don't praise and worship God because He needs it. We praise and worship because we need it. When we praise God, we become aligned with Him and enable Him to work in our lives.

Make a list of ten things for which you can thank God.

Try phoning or writing someone and tell them something really cool that God did or that you like about God.

Did you feel a shift in the atmosphere around you?

Chapter 15

Master Choreographer

Who comforts us in all our troubles,
so that we can comfort those in any trouble
with the comfort we ourselves receive from God.

2 CORINTHIANS 1:4, NIV

I continued making video productions from 1993 to 2008—more than 15 years. In 2008, we produced the last one, *Dancing with God*. It was life-transforming for everyone involved.

People from four cultures participated: First Nations, Chinese, African and Filipino. Each group was given the same four songs to choreograph according to their culture, but none had knowledge of how the others would represent these songs in dance. The choreographers had never met, but when we filmed and edited, we were astounded to discover that in the choruses their movements matched exactly. It is clear that the Holy Spirit was the master choreographer, and the result was powerful.

When giftings blend, there is unity and blessing. We saw this principle at work a few years ago when Lana, another worship dance instructor, and I were invited to teach in Costa Rica. We were the only two out of six teachers who arrived. The organizers had to revise the entire program to arrange for us to share the workshops.

Both Lana and I sought the Lord on which workshops each of us should take. The students saw that we deferred to each other, preferred one another and truly wanted God's leading. The organizer was pleased with how well we flowed together in the Spirit and felt our co-operation was a good model of Christ for the students. As a result, we were invited back to do more conferences in Costa Rica and Nicaragua.

COMPETE OR COMPLETE

When we allow the Spirit to lead, instead of competing, we complete each other, the way my friend who runs a technical dance studio in Oakville, Ontario, and I do.

Heidi Knapp teaches technical dance. As an instructor she is highly in demand across the country. She is also a very good examiner. When we work together, we complete each other. She teaches the technical aspects of dance, and I teach the spiritual. Together it's a perfect fit and flow in the Holy Spirit.

Heidi and I were introduced at a performance at the Living Arts Centre in Mississauga. I was training a group of 60 church people who had never danced, and she had seven highly accomplished technical dancers. When we saw what the other was doing, we loved it, and we began working together.

My dancers, waving flags, surrounded her girls in the performance. They complemented each other, and we sensed a strong presence and favour of God on our work. I am always prepared to work with Heidi because there is never competition between us. It's also refreshing that her focus is on the Lord rather than on self-promotion. Both of us want to see God's work done, regardless of who does it.

WAIST DEEP

It's exciting and fulfilling to watch the Holy Spirit minister when we yield, step aside and allow Him to move. One of the most powerful ministry tools He uses through this ministry is my workshop River of Healing. It's less an invention of mine than an intervention by God in my life. He was there when I needed Him. This is what happened.

I was sitting by the mouth of a river in British Columbia, feeling heavy laden. I was writing in my journal, pouring out my heart on paper to the Lord and naming the things from which I wanted release. When I was done, I ripped the pages from my journal one by one, scrunched them up and threw them in the river. I watched their tranquil bobbing on the water before me.

Just then a breeze swept past me, caught my journal pages and pro-pelled them gently along the water's surface away from me and out to sea.

I leapt up. An irrational alarm seized me. My heart had been very open in the things I had written. As the pages floated away, I felt transparent. Exposed! *Oh, oh! I don't want anyone to read this!* I thought.

It didn't occur to me that they would get waterlogged and sink. I kicked off my shoes and ran into the water after them, wading as fast as I could, water splashing, ankle deep, knee deep! I stretched out to catch them, but the pages, as if teasing me, stayed just out of reach. Waist deep! I could go no farther. I stopped and watched. Carried swiftly on a gust, they blew away. I had to let them go.

When I released them, I was immediately aware that something in me changed. I felt a powerful presence, a closeness, a oneness with God. The burdens I had written on the papers lifted off me and blew away with them. I experienced a healing miracle. I was healed in the river!

I recalled how my leg was healed in the river of life with Jesus. I knew that throughout Scripture God uses the imagery of water to identify His presence. Ezekiel speaks about the river of life that heals: "Wherever the river flows...everything...will live" (Ezekiel 47:9, NIV). Jesus stood in the temple and announced that He is the river "of living water" (John 7:38, NLT). We are also to be baptized—immersed in the living water of God.

MAKE-BELIEVE RIVER

My river experience took place in summer. Now it was winter and I was back in Ontario. I had more "stuff" to deal with, and I was crying out to God. I desperately wanted the healing river again, but it was freezing outside. *I can't wait till summer,* I complained to Him. *I have to get rid of this, and the bathtub won't do. Where can I get a river?*

A picture of blue fabric popped into my mind, and it occurred to me that it could be a metaphor for water. I went to the fabric store, bought yards of blue material, laid it out on my living room floor and converted it into a winding make-believe river.

I sat looking at my "river," crying and writing out my unresolved issues. Big pillows at the "mouth" of my river served as rocks. I scrunched the papers, tucked them under the pillows and stepped into the river.

I walked by faith, deep in the Spirit. Sure enough, the burdens I had been carrying lifted. I reached the end of the river, threw the papers in the fireplace to burn, and was free. Thinking that people might consider me foolish, I determined not to tell anyone about my experience.

THE MANTLE

Around that time I was invited to speak at a women's retreat in northern Ontario. I knew I wasn't to go, but I didn't know how to turn down the invitation. That night I had a dream.

In the dream I was at the retreat, sitting on a couch. Jesus came to me, reached down and took something off me and put something else on. "You're wearing the wrong mantle," He said. He raised His arm and pointed south. I understood His gesture. I wasn't to be here. I should be ministering elsewhere. I woke up thinking, *I can't go to that retreat.*

That morning at 8:00, a pastor called. She was crying. "We need healing in our church. Has the Lord given you anything new lately?" I knew her well and felt comfortable to share my river experience but wasn't sure it would help her church.

"Belma. That's it! That's exactly what we need!" she exclaimed.

Great peace and assurance descended on me. I knew right away that this was the direction in which Jesus had pointed. I felt the mantle envelope me, and knew He intended for me to use the river in ministry.

Along with the fabric, a waterfall, rocks, the riverbank, basins of water and the cross, it took more than five hours to lay out the river. I hadn't thought of using the fabric river as a ministry tool, but now I was sure it was God's will. The results at this first booking were dramatic. The pastors felt God "came through big time." The healing they needed took place.

Since then, whenever I minister the River of Healing workshop I share my story, tell people to write down the burdens they need to release, and encourage them to walk the river to the cross. Word spread that people were set free, and more invitations came.

Usually I do ministry first at my church before taking it elsewhere, but this time my pastor heard about it from others. "You have to do this at our church," he said. When I did, people were powerfully touched and healed. One older man testified, "I felt compelled to get on my hands and knees and crawl to the cross. The Lord told me to do it. I feel so clean!"

TRANSFORMATION

Not long after, a group of us received an invitation from a First Nations pastor to fly to a southern Alberta reserve. We went as a team of seven pastors and me. I set up the river, and when I invited people to walk it, many came, but three women balked. They represented three generations: gramma, daughter, and granddaughter. All three stood screaming, wailing and crying at the beginning of the river. They put one foot in, took it out. Put another foot in, took it out. Unable to step into the river, they did this for 45 minutes. Finally, when they began to walk, with each step they shook, wailed in grief and clung to each other for support, and they stopped many times to cry and rest on each other's shoulders. But they made it through. It took them two and a half hours.

There was a marked change in the women when they reached the end of the river. Their faces beamed. They were free, filled with joy and laughter, sharing an infectious happiness they had never before experienced. In their new-found freedom their steps were light, as if their feet were on holy ground. Both gramma and daughter shared stories of devastation in their families.

They both had lost their husbands, one by suicide and one by murder, their bodies swept away in the current of an actual river on their property.

It was surreal to hear their story. I felt a deep sadness for them and was grateful that I didn't know the circumstances before I asked them to walk the river. I was even more grateful that they had conquered it. Along with everyone, I was in awe, but I also marvelled at God's omniscience. I felt so small before Him, realizing I was a participant in His will, His leading, His ministry and His plan.

Pause and Reflect

People strive to be "somebody" to prove their value. They don't realize that they already have value in Christ. When you know who you are in Christ and you move in His gifting, your actions are worship to Him.

How is the act of performing to receive value or self-esteem different than the act of performing as a worshipper of God?

We don't have value through popularity. We are valuable to the extent that God is glorified through our lives. The Holy Spirit always glorifies Jesus, not the individual seeking fame. God blesses Belma's ministry because she rejects self-promotion. She may be tempted to enjoy attention, but from a pure heart she turns the glory back to God.

Sometimes, the enemy plants thoughts in us in hopes we'll accept them as if they were our own. Through flattery he draws us away from God to glorify ourselves.

Name some TV shows that are built on self-promotion. What do their titles suggest to you?

Think of famous people who have struggled under the weight of stardom. Would you say that fame and fortune are easy taskmasters?

Chapter 16

Blessed

The Spirit of the Sovereign LORD is on me, because the LORD has anointed me to proclaim good news to the poor. He has sent me to bind up the brokenhearted, to proclaim freedom for the captives and release from darkness for the prisoners, to proclaim the year of the LORD's favor.

ISAIAH 61:1–2, NIV

God assures all who suffer deep pain that He will raise them out of ashes of despair into beauty and joy. He will pour out blessing on them until they are filled with praise and stand strong in righteousness before Him.

Those are His words to me. That promise is fulfilled in my life.

I believe that the grace of God that flows through this ministry is rooted in the ability God gave me to forgive my mother. Out of the pain I experienced, I can now comfort others with His love and understanding.

Since I forgave my mother, God has arranged for me to fly all over the world with Celebration of Dance. He has not only given me the finances to do it, but He has provided blessings I could have never imagined. He treats me like royalty. I was amazed once when a white limo met me at the airport. "Who is that for?" I asked.

"It's for you! You are the bride of Christ!" someone replied.

At whatever church God sends me to, the pastor and his wife become my family. We always have an instant intimate connection because God has arranged for me to work with them. When I arrive I ask them to share the vision they have for involving me in their ministry. I ask what the Lord has shown them, because I need to be on board with what they're doing.

One afternoon at a church in Montreal the leadership dragged me away from teaching, to a mall. They spent $3,000 on new clothes for me. They said I looked a bit outdated. My clothes still felt new to me, but then I realized that I might have bought them ten years before. Clothes shopping just isn't my priority.

Churches have been very generous to me. One congregation bought me a Mac computer. I hadn't even mentioned that I needed one. This type of provision recurs wherever I go. My needs are always met, and usually God does more than I could ask or think.

When I arrived in Cranbrook, B.C., a welcoming party greeted me with a big sign that read "Welcome Belma Vardy! Hallelujah!" Everyone hugged me. "We painted your bedroom purple and we got a purple bedspread and purple flowers because we feel like we are receiving royalty," they said.

My heart melted. I am blessed!

I'M BLESSED

I love this ministry. It's great fun to see someone experience a breakthrough with God. I'm happiest when I'm doing things for the Lord and seeing them benefit God's kingdom. But I can get so focused on ministry that I forget to relax and have fun the way people normally do. Doing "fun" things can sometimes even seem like a waste of time. I think this attitude is partially rooted in my childhood. Even though I have forgiven my mother, the way she treated me affected me on many levels. When I lived with her I wasn't allowed playtime with friends, but God is changing that.

Over the years I have had to learn to take a break from ministry and relax with friends. It reminds me of an incident at a church where I was teaching for three weeks. The pastor said, "Let's take Monday off and have a 'fun' day." He and his wife took me to an amusement park to enjoy the rides. We almost had the whole park to ourselves. I enjoyed their fellowship as much as the rides, and the three of us really had a rich "fun" day together.

My stories of blessings through churches are endless. I never know what will happen.

Once I was dancing at a pastors' conference. At one point I twirled in my dress, which had 20 metres of fabric just in the skirt. A woman came to me afterwards and said, "When you twirled, I saw my three grandchildren. They were in the dress, and the dress became the hands of Jesus." Then she shared that her grandchildren had died. "But now I know they are with Jesus," she added.

The pastors expressed their appreciation that the design of my outfit wasn't suggestive and didn't distract people from entering into God's presence.

MODESTY IN MINISTRY

There is sacredness in a dance before the Lord by a woman appropriately dressed. Her outfit contributes to the ability of people to connect with God. The design must not give the enemy an opportunity to draw people's attention away from worship into lust. For this reason, a dancer must not wear suggestive attire. A dancer should not draw attention to her body. As long as she is modestly attired, people can focus on the Lord.

A prime example occurred when Mary Audrey and I were invited to minister in a northern British Columbia logging town. We were participating in a women's conference. I arrived a week before Mary Audrey to prepare the children and youth for their part in the conference. During that week I heard rumblings that the men, most of whom were lumberjacks, felt left out. The church, unwilling that any should be discontent, asked me to work on spiritual awakening with the men as well.

We arranged a men's workshop. I taught them a song with choreography using flags in the formation of Canada geese. This formation looks like an arrow and can symbolize piercing the darkness.

The men tried, but they were very shaky and off-beat. The presentation didn't resemble any Canada geese formation anyone had ever seen. It seemed to me that something was not aligned spiritually. I went to the pastor and explained, "We need you as a leader. This isn't going to work without you."

The Holy Spirit must have stirred him because he joined us right away. We tried our Canada geese formation again with him right at the front of the "V" to lead the men. Immediately it came into perfect alignment and stability. What happened?

The pastor, formerly in the army, had been trained in discipline, leadership and marching. He was the missing "lead goose." He understood the steps and the importance of walking in unity. As the men submitted under the pastor's leadership, the formation came together. "You need your leader to keep the flow going," I told them. I saw a broader application as well: when we submit under leadership, there's unity.

At the end of the workshop we prayed together. During our corporate prayer, the Holy Spirit touched the men with repentance. In tears, one by one they confessed their sins before God. I prayed for each one as they poured out their hearts. They must have felt safe with me, but I felt awkward with the things they were confessing.

When prayer time ended, they were still in tears. I didn't understand what had moved them so deeply. "It's not fair," one said. "We're the spiritual leaders in our homes, but we don't get training for it. It's a lot to deal with. Women get the conferences and teaching, and we're left to figure it out ourselves." I felt compassion for them and understood their need. Later, when I approached the leadership, they decided to include the men.

During the conference, Mary Audrey spoke about the significance of horses in the spiritual realm. She put chairs on the stage with their backs to the people. Mary Audrey, the pastor and I sat backwards on the chairs facing the people. The pastor called on them to turn their chairs around as well and sit on them backwards with their hands on the chair backs as if they were riding horses. A funny thing happened.

One of the men spontaneously climbed onto the shoulders of another man as if he were riding a horse. He snapped his flag and cheered as they galloped around the gym. Their happy display created a change in the onlookers. It drew forth the "heart of the child" in everyone, and joy broke out in the congregation.

When the conference ended, the men reported feeling stronger. Their hope was renewed, and they were prepared to go home and be spiritual leaders.

I can't explain what God does or why He does it, but I am grateful to work alongside Him to set His people free. It's intriguing to me that I, as a female, could carry God's anointing to a room full of macho lumberjacks and not detract them from their purpose of drawing closer to God. The men were so unaffected by my femininity that they could confess their deepest sins in my presence and the Holy Spirit could create a safe place for them to share who they really were.

Let me share another example.

In Minnesota I was introducing worship dance to a church where many men were pig farmers. Regardless of whether I am up north with lumberjacks or down south with farmers, as men see and appreciate this "new" form of worship, they want it and want more of the Lord. They want to get in on what God is doing.

That is what happened with the farmers. As they saw the joy in the women, children and youth who were taking the classes, they came to me with a hunger for God in their eyes. One of them put his hands on both my shoulders, looked me straight in the eyes and said, "Please can you teach us?"

It was so difficult for me to turn them down, but I had to say, "You have the schedule. You know I have no time left. I'm only here for two weeks, and I'm busy teaching from sunup to sundown."

"What about during your lunchtime?" one asked.

I was tired and needed my lunch hours, but they were desperate. In the end I didn't have to give it up. We agreed to meet at 8:00 in the morning. They wanted to keep our meetings a secret from their wives so their presentation would be a surprise. Their wives, they said, would think they were feeding the pigs at that time.

We had a great time together. I taught them a warrior dance. We waved flags and did a song with very militant moves.

I also introduced them to the "Intimacy with God" workshop. God's Spirit really moved among them.

While they were worshipping in a circle, the Lord said, "Put two flags at the pastor's feet." Later the pastor shared what happened to him.

He had been worshipping with his eyes shut when he heard the Lord say, "Son, pick up the flags."

"I don't have any flags," he responded, but the Lord said, "Open your eyes and look down at your feet." There they were. He picked up the flags and made unusual movements. He looked silly. I had to look away because I didn't want him to see me watching. I felt embarrassed for him at what I saw him doing through my peripheral vision.

He continued his testimony. In a vision, he was at the end of a runway. God told him to flag in the incoming planes. Along came a big 747. "Son, I want you to land it right there at the end of that runway," God said.

He waved the flags furiously to get that plane down. When it landed, the door opened. His eyes welled up as he spoke. "Out walked the King of Glory. He came toward me, put His hands on my face and said, 'Well done, my faithful servant.'" Now all of us were misty. In tears, the others in the workshop shared their experiences as well.

On Sunday morning the men met me early again, still secretly. They were ready with their presentation.

THIS IS CHURCH

Word got out that the whole church would be dancing, and the whole town wanted to see the spectacle. It had become a big deal in this part of rural Minnesota. Several other churches had cancelled their services to see our presentations. The church was packed: grandmas, grandpas, aunts, uncles, cousins—everybody came.

I was scheduled to open with my testimony. According to the program, when I was done a woman was to blow the shofar to begin the festivities, and the women were to launch into jubilant praise with tambourines. Instead, we arranged a surprise. I had instructed the men differently.

At the end of my speech I announced, "Will the warriors get into their positions, please?" The men took their cue, the doors flew open and they marched down the aisles, triumphantly waving flags.

I watched the reactions of the women. They looked at each other in disbelief. I could hear their whispers: "What's your husband doing there?"

"Look, there's *your* husband!"

"Wait a minute—that's *my* husband!"

It was a delight to see. Movement almost seemed slow motion. The women stood staring at their warriors marching before them. Everybody was thrilled. The hall erupted in cheers that rivalled a football game as they marched out. It united all the denominations present. They were ready to receive whatever God had for them.

At the end of the service we waved the flags of all nations. The scene stirred deep patriotism in people's hearts, and they took it in with reverence. There was silence. The entire congregation was moved by God's presence. The pastor looked at me. *Now what?* I wondered, thinking he should close the meeting.

BANG! BANG! BANG! The noise shook everyone out of their reverie. An old woman in a wheelchair was banging her cane on the floor and trying to move forward. "I want the microphone," she bellowed. The pastor handed it to her. "I've been going to this church for 86 years," she hollered, "and I just want to say, *this is church!*"

The church exploded into cheers and applause again. It was wonderful, wild and fulfilling all at the same time. We were wrapped in the electrifying presence of God.

As a sidenote, the woman who blew the shofar received emotional healing. Years earlier when her father was ill, she had hoped he would be healed when she blew her shofar. It didn't happen. He died, and she had not touched the instrument since—until the day of our performance. People were aware of her story and rejoiced to see her victory over grief.

For 31 years, whenever I come home from engagements I feel like I've been in another world. And I guess I have. Every booking has its special moments. Church is never boring, and ministry responsibility, never a trial. It has been an adventure, especially since God began to send me frequently to minister to First Nations people.

Pause and Reflect

It's not possible to serve both God and *mammon* (the Greek term for "money, wealth and material possessions"). Belma put God's will ahead of money.

Would you say that your life up to this point has been led by the need for mammon or by the need to know you are doing the will of God?

When we're in ministry, doing relaxing things can seem like a waste of time, but sometimes it's God's way of ministering to us. We need refreshing. God wants more than work from us. Sometimes God just wants us to enjoy His presence and calls us to get away for relaxation and rest.

When was the last time you kicked up your heels and had a deep belly laugh or just lay on a beach and enjoyed the quiet?

Are you able to enjoy the presence of God when you are relaxing or enjoying a hobby, or do you feel a sense of guilt?

The next time you take some time out, try taking Jesus with you and sense the difference.

Chapter 17

Where the River Flows

Where the river flows everything will live.

EZEKIEL 47:9, NIV

L et me share some of my interactions with First Nations tribes. In 2009 I was in Ness Lake, B.C., taking part in a ladies' conference. About 300 women attended. Most were First Nations women who had come from great distances. Thirty were from the Bella Coola reserve in B.C.'s far north. These women had spent three months in a garbage dump, searching for salvageable things they could sell to raise money for gas to get to the conference. It was a long drive. By God's grace they raised the money and arrived in vans.

When I shared my story, many cried as they relived it with me. "You are one of us," they said. They related to me being taken from my childhood home, losing my parents, living in harsh circumstances and trying to understand a strange language. One woman shared her experience in the "Movement and Intimacy" workshop: "I've been married 38 years to the same man. We have eight children. In all the years of marriage, my husband has never given me a hug. Today I feel I have received a hug from Jesus."

It thrills me to hear stories of Jesus stepping in to heal. Their spirits (hearts, according to Scripture) have been crushed and broken. God, in His power, reaches deep to restore. From a restoration of the spirit, healing flows to the soul: mind, will and emotions. The whole person changes. No well-meaning social program can offer healing such as this.

I still marvel at how God opened doors for me to bring my story to many of the First Nations tribes in the most unexpected way. It just demonstrates that our smallest obedience in response to His command can yield the greatest results. Let me share an incident that happened after the conference.

A GIFT

A woman who had attended called me, asking to order three of my videos. I learned at the post office that the cost of shipping would be seventeen dollars. With money in short supply, it seemed too much to spend on postage. Apparently cost didn't faze God. That evening He told me to send fifty videos, no charge, as a gift. What to do? Knowing my thoughts, God added, "I'll pay for the shipping."

I took my box of fifty videos to the post office and asked how much it would be. The answer: thirty-one dollars and fifty cents.

"How can that be?" I asked in surprise. "Three videos are seventeen dollars, but fifty are thirty-one fifty?"

"When you send more, the price comes down," the clerk answered.

I was delighted. "Well then, I'm just going to believe for a rich businessman to pay for shipping."

As I picked up my box to take home, the clerk, who was a Christian, came around from the desk, took my hand and pressed a twenty dollar bill into it. "Here," she said. "This is toward postage."

"Wait! Wait!" cried another clerk. "Don't leave me out! I want to contribute too."

She retrieved her purse and emptied her wallet. "Oh no! My husband took all my money!" she exclaimed in dismay. "All I have is eleven fifty."

We gasped! Realizing what had just happened, we looked at each other in wonder. "Eleven fifty and twenty dollars is thirty-one fifty!" I cried. "That covers it!" The three of us jumped up and down, rejoicing like children.

I phoned the woman in Bella Coola and told her what God had done. "I sent you a box of fifty, and there is no charge! Take your three videos and ask the Lord what to do with the rest."

AN INVITATION

Two weeks later she called. "The videos arrived. I gave them out, and the Bella Coola women are dancing in their homes. We're wondering, would you come teach us if you were invited?"

I had only met these women once, at the conference at Ness Lake, but without hesitation I said yes.

The woman continued. "Protocol requires for you to be invited by the Chief."

I wasn't worried. "If the Lord wants me there, He'll speak to the Chief. Just don't push anything. I don't want to go unless the Lord opens the door."

Another week and a half later, she called very excited. She had gone to see the Chief, who was a born-again Spirit-filled believer. "When I went in," she said, "he was sitting with his arms folded in front of him, praying. I said, 'Chief Noel, I need to speak to you about a woman named Belma Vardy.' He said, 'The Lord has already spoken to me about Belma. She is to come here and teach you women. Go. Tell her to book her flight.'"

WELCOME

I was astounded and delighted at God's clear directive. Correct protocol requires that when a Chief invites one to a reserve, one cannot say no, but to observe custom and good manners, one never goes without an invitation.

Protocol also required that I call the Chief with my request. I highly respected his authority and hoped my words would convey my heart. "Chief Noel," I began. "I understand that God spoke to you about me coming to Bella Coola to share with your women. I am calling to request permission to teach on your land."

His response humbled me. "I want to welcome you into our territory. You will be a blessing. We are thankful that you are coming. Go by His direction, not mine."

We talked for three hours. Chief Noel spoke at length about many things. The history of his tribe and the pain they suffered from their interactions with non-Indigenous was foremost on his mind. He told me that deep rejection runs in the hearts of his people.

RIVER OF HEALING

How could I have imagined, when I stood in the post office with a box of 50 videos, that it would open the doors for me to arrive in Bella Coola with 50 pounds of blue fabric to minister the River of Healing workshop? The plane landed on Anahim Lake's one little runway, surrounded by mountains. I had been instructed to get off and wait at the end of the gravel road. A school bus picked me up. The ride to Bella Coola took three and a half hours.

During my stay on the reserve, Chief Noel escorted me into the Band House, where all historical records are kept, where the chiefs hold council meetings and where important decisions are made. It is not a place where outsiders, especially non-Indigenous women, are invited. I was humbled that the Chief trusted me.

In Bella Coola I laid the blue fabric on the floor throughout the room to create the river of healing. The congregation listened to my story and, with God's help, relived injustices they had suffered. They walked the river of healing crying, repenting and forgiving. At the cross they released their pains to Jesus, and His blood washed them away. The people received great freedom and asked for the river ministry again on the Sunday morning before I left.

The River of Healing workshop was particularly helpful to the youth because they could express their pains and sorrows on paper and share them only with God as they walked the river.

A workshop on freedom through dance was also liberating for them. They received such personal freedom that on the last night I was there, they led their community in a dance that exploded with such joy that they even pulled adults out of their seats to participate.

Upon my departure, two chiefs each presented me with an eagle feather—the highest honour. They invited me to return anytime, saying, "This is your home."

It never ceases to amaze me that my story opens doors to these wonderful but isolated communities. After the Bella Coola experience, word travelled quickly to other chiefs and councils. As a result, I was invited to four more northern Canadian reserves. As is common for many of these remote communities, they were not accessible by car. One, for instance, required four flights, and the farther north, the smaller the planes. Some required 14 hours of flying time or 14 hours of driving on logging roads.

HISTORY 101

Since then, I have had many other opportunities to share with First Nations people. In 2010, I spoke at a pastors' conference in Ontario and also ministered the River of Healing workshop. Some pastors in attendance were from Manitoulin Island, and they invited me to minister there. I sensed once again the Lord's leading and agreed to go.

I knew it would be a special experience when Jerry, a retired police officer, met me at the airport with a big handmade sign, "Welcome Belma Vardy!" He took me on what became a seven-hour guided First Nations "History 101" tour from Sudbury to Manitoulin Island. Our final stop was South Baymouth. Pastors had requested a dance camp for Indigenous children, who were picked up from a nearby reserve for church every Sunday.

As we drove, Jerry poured out his heart. He shared how the government had indoctrinated him, along with countless others, including many First Nations people, to believe that he would be doing good by helping remove select children from their homes and flying them to residential schools. Jerry shared how he personally believed it would benefit the children, the reservation, and the First Nations to do so. He told how in every community the children had been fascinated with the "big bird landing from the sky." Most had never seen a plane. Some had been prepared to go and left willingly, but most were lured onto the planes with candy. For them it was a difficult departure.

As time passed, however, it became clear to Jerry that harm came to not only the children but their families, their communities and their culture. When he realized that he had knowingly and willingly inflicted harm on them, it cut him deeply. He still struggles to make restitution. "I've taken every opportunity to pay back and make up for what I had done. I volunteered in First Nations communities, worked with troubled youth, and mentored families in crisis...I still haven't paid the debt I owe these people," he said.

MISSING

Out of many stories he could share, Jerry chose to tell about an incident that liberated a young girl. A resident of one of the First Nations Reserves had called the police and reported his 11-year-old daughter missing. The police searched, but she was nowhere to be found. Neither did they have any trace of evidence to follow.

One night, however, Jerry sensed the Lord telling him to go to a specific house and check inside a closet. While apprehensive, he followed the prompting, and he found the missing girl. Nausea overwhelmed him. For three and a half years she had been locked in the closet and abused: forced to eat, sleep and relieve herself there. Her mental and physical growth had been stunted.

As we drove, Jerry recounted story after agonizing story of a lifestyle inherent to poverty and rampant discrimination. He pointed out a place where a First Nations mother in deep despair had drowned herself and her two boys. This type of incident, he stated, was not unique to First Nations people.

Eventually we arrived at the camp. The minister's wife met us and introduced me to the kids. A woman among them, who looked to be about 30 years old, was very sweet but somewhat slow mentally. She seemed attracted to me and stayed close, assisting me all week. She carried flags and did many little tasks to help.

At the end of the week, the kids presented a dance. After the performance Jerry came to me. "I didn't want to tell you before, but the girl you befriended was the one I found in the closet years ago. You have been so kind to her. She sees you as her newest friend. Had I told you, you may have treated her differently. I saw how she was drawn to you and how you loved her."

THE FAR NORTH

On another occasion, I was in Kangiqsujuaq, a little village of 600 people in northernmost Quebec just south of Baffin Island, on the beautiful tundra of the far north. To reach the community, it requires seven flights northward from Montreal. The village is on the Hudson Strait, and the only way to get there is by air. If the weather is bad, it's impossible to access.

At the time Kuujjuaq, farther south, was home to a tiny one-room airport on the tree line. It was the hub for all the little villages of the far north. It was a collection point for the flight to Montreal, and there was only one a day. On my way back I encountered so many delays that I missed that flight.

I tried to arrange another flight and asked where I could stay overnight. The attendant shrugged. Just like in the biblical story, there was no room at the inn. The hotel was so full, people were sleeping on the floor in the laundry room.

"Fine," I said. "I'll stay in the airport."

"You can't," she retorted. "We close at six."

I was beginning to think I would have to sleep outside when an Air Inuit employee offered me her apartment. She would find somewhere else to sleep.

I was grateful. Air Inuit also gave me coupons for the only restaurant in town. The flight would be the next afternoon at five o'clock. I imagined having a whole day to rest, relax and read my Bible. Wonderful! This would be a great layover after all.

I was enjoying dinner when an Inuit woman came into the restaurant, noticed me and said, "I know you!"

I recognized her too. In 1995, she and a group of Inuit women had attended one of my sessions at Singing Waters Christian Retreat Centre near Orangeville, Ontario.

"A Christian up here! Wonderful!" she exclaimed.

The next morning at breakfast, there she was again. We were excited to connect with each other. "I want to show you my town!" she announced.

I realized that the Lord had other plans for me that day than relaxing, so I agreed.

THE RINGMASTER

I had noticed many people going into a building down the street and asked my newly appointed tour guide what was happening there. "It's a government building," she said. "I work there. The crowd is there to see Cirque du Soleil."

People farther north had mentioned Cirque du Soleil. Some were auditioning their kids. Cirque du Soleil trained them and took the good ones as performers. When I heard about this, I mentioned that I would love to train in one of their workshops. I hoped for some pointers on teaching kids.

We entered the building, and my friend told the receptionist I wanted to participate in a workshop. The girl summoned the ringmaster. "I hear you teach dance," he said. "Can you teach a workshop for us this morning?"

I quickly corrected him. "Oh no! I just want to sit in on one and watch how you teach."

"No way!" he insisted, "We want *you* to teach!"

I had 15 minutes to prepare. I rushed to the apartment, rummaged through my stuff, found some music, and hurried back to Cirque du Soleil. *Lord*, I breathed silently, *I need a word from You!* I had no idea what music I should use or what I should teach. I had to hear from God.

PHARAOH, PHARAOH

They gave me a group of little boys ages eight, nine and ten. To find their level of creativity, I assigned a partner to each boy and asked them to make a statue of their partner that expressed their culture or beliefs. "I'm non-Indigenous," I explained. "I want to learn about you."

The first little boy shared that his partner was holding a big bucket full of the blood of Jesus. Jesus had said there was enough blood in the bucket to pour out on everyone in the room, and He wanted to pour it out on them.

His response took away my breath. He was God's confirmation that I was in the right place at the right time.

I taught the group many songs. They particularly liked a lively tune, "Pharaoh, Pharaoh." The ringmaster decided that would be the one.

"Before we learn this song, we need to know what it means, where it comes from and why we're doing it," he told the kids. Turning to me, he asked, "Could you please tell us what 'Pharaoh, Pharaoh' is about?"

"It's from the Bible," I explained. "For you to understand it, I have to read the Bible story."

"Great! Everybody sit down," ordered the ringmaster. "We're going to hear a story."

There I was, reading the Bible to Cirque du Soleil. Originally I was to teach one workshop, but it became three, four, then five. They practiced the song with gusto: "Ooo, ooo—let my people go...Yeah, yeah, yeah, yeah..."

I eventually learned that "Pharaoh, Pharaoh" became part of Cirque de Soleil's repertoire for years to come.

I taught all day. My flight was leaving at 5:20 p.m., and I was supposed to check in at 4:00. I called the airport. "I'm still here teaching, but I have to go to the apartment and get my stuff."

"Don't worry! We'll come pick you up," said the airline employee. We rushed to the apartment, stuffed everything into my bags and dashed to the airport. It was crazy! Check-in was a blur—they bypassed security and shoved me onto the plane. As the engines roared and the plane tilted for liftoff, I laid my head against the back of the seat and smiled, echoes of "Pharaoh, Pharaoh" still in my mind. I basked in God's presence—full, satisfied and complete.

I wouldn't trade this life for anything!

FULL CIRCLE

God put the drive to live, be loved and belong deep inside me, and it has come full circle. I now enjoy the warmth, love, affirmation and special friendships of an extended family far beyond any I could have imagined—more mothers, dads, brothers and sisters than I ever thought possible. All of them are precious gifts that make up for the years of pain and emptiness—dear friends and family whom I love, and who love me.

At the same time I find life, not in things but in a fulfilling ministry of sharing, teaching, dancing, producing worship dance videos and releasing God's life to others. I couldn't be happier.

The circle of my life is complete, and with deepest gratitude I acknowledge that it was only possible *because God was there.*

Pause and Reflect

Belma thought God wanted her to rest during her layover, but it turned out that He had a different plan. What a good example of how we can be completely wrong! The best adventures come when we listen to the Holy Spirit and follow His leading. He takes us on a very exciting minute by minute, day by day, hour by hour journey.

Have you ever followed through on an impression that seemed a bit random (such as to phone someone out of the blue or walk down a certain street) but turned out quite wonderful?

Make it your business over the next few weeks to have as many God-adventures as you can!

Epilogue

BY LORNE SHEPHERD

As a little girl, Belma expressed a desire to meet Jesus. She told her grandmother once that she would have loved to be alive in the time of Jesus. I believe God heard her cry, sustained her and became her father, mother, brother, and sister in her darkest hours. He transformed the abuse that could have destroyed her into ministry gifts and a passion and love for God and people. Her personal praise-and-worship dance, as well as her ability to train children, youth and adults all over the world to perform powerfully in praise and worship, is a beautiful expression of this love.

The story begins in wartime Germany. The war had a marked effect not only on Belma but also on her mother, who became a very wounded, troubled, bitter and angry woman because she was never healed from the abuse. As a result, she hurt and abused others, especially those with whom she needed to be in relationship.

It wasn't an accident that Belma lived with her grandparents in her formative years. God knew what she would have to face in the future. Her grandparents loved her. She bonded with them and learned how to love. She saw how her grandma and grandpa coped with circumstances and watched them depend on God. In spite of the difficulties of life, they imparted to Belma the ability to hope, trust and forgive. Together they faced troubled times knowing that God loved them and that they loved one another.

God answers every little child who wants to know Him and calls out to Him. He never leaves them. He has a purpose for them. We see this illustrated in Belma's story. Even though her mother was evil, manipulative and narcissistic, God preserved Belma. She chose to forgive and co-operate with Jesus, and therefore He could redeem her life and turn the abuse, neglect and rejection into blessing.

Belma is like many children who have suffered much, but because she allowed Jesus to transform her life, she is now able to be a blessing to thousands all over the world.

It's never too late to bring your woundedness and suffered injustices to Jesus, lay them at His feet and let Him be your father, mother, brother and sister. He will transform your journey.

It's not an accident that you read this book. God knows your story. We hope this book encourages you and gives you hope to see that you don't have to be tied to injustices of the past regardless of what has happened to you.

God has always been there for you, as much as He was for Belma. He has especially been there in your darkest hours when you have felt most alone. God hasn't forgotten you. Trust in Him, and you will see Him turn every trial into a victory.

Jesus said that every hair on your head is numbered by God (Matthew 10:30). Nothing has happened to you that He did not feel personally. He died for you and others like you.

You have a purpose. "'For I know the plans I have for you,' declares the LORD, 'plans to prosper you and not to harm you, plans to give you hope and a future'" (Jeremiah 29:11, NIV).

Your life has meaning. God is calling you to come. It's never too late. "Come to me, all you who are weary and burdened, and I will give you rest" (Matthew 11:28, NIV).

Will you give Him your life? Your past? Your future? Your journey? You'll never be the same again!

Discussion and Study Guide

BY BECKY THOMAS

This "Discussion and Study Guide" is intended for small groups. The purpose of the questions is to help lift our eyes off of our own hearts and perspectives to find God's heart and perspective in all circumstances—our personal lives, families, communities and nations. Coming to know His heart made all the difference for Belma, and it will make all the difference for you.

Whether you are using this individually or as part of a group, do not feel the need to answer all the questions at once, but focus on the ones that seem to "capture" the work God is doing in you at the time of reading. You will notice that there are lots of questions to consider as the book moves on. You can come back to these anytime. You will find that the Lord may highlight a different set as you dig deeper and deeper into His heart and perspective.

Before you begin, may we suggest you take a few minutes to meditate on the chapters' opening Scriptures. Feel free to journal and ask the Lord to speak to you through the verses.

CHAPTER 1: TERROR IN THE NIGHT

"He will cover you with his feathers, and under his wings you will find refuge...You will not fear the terror of night, nor the arrow that flies by day." (Psalm 91:4–5, NIV)

1. On the world's political stage many "secrets" have been kept from public scrutiny. Yet those secrets affect real people living today. *Can you think of some modern day "secrets" that need to be addressed?*

2. *How do you think the hiding and the secrecy in Belma's childhood may have affected her emotionally? Can you describe a scene in your own life— an instance when you felt the need to be hidden?*

3. Oma and Opa represented safety to Belma. *Describe the place where you feel most safe. What made or makes it a safe place for you?*

4. Belma remembers being *mein kleines Schätzchen* to Oma and Opa. *Is there someone or something that makes you feel precious? What made you feel so?*

CHAPTER 2: BEGINNINGS

"If the LORD had not been my help, my soul would soon have lived in the land of silence." (Psalm 94:17, ESV)

1. In Psalm 139:13 the songwriter talks about being knit together in our mother's womb. Belma experienced divine protection when her mother tried to abort her. *Recall a time in your life when you may have experienced divine protection or guidance.*

2. Belma's vision included a scene where God placed His hand upon babies, saying, "These ones need a special blessing because they are unwanted. They have been rejected and will have much rejection." *What does this say to you about the value God places on the unwanted and unloved?*

3. Belma states, "After we were blessed, Jesus walked us back and re-turned us into the womb, but He didn't leave." *What does this speak to you about God's involvement and role with people? Have you ever been aware of His presence with you?*

4. *How does Belma's vision affect the way you view your own life? Are you aware of His blessing on your existence?*

CHAPTER 3: ROOTED IN LOVE

"For my father and my mother have forsaken me, but the LORD will take me in." (Psalm 27:10, ESV)

1. In this chapter we see things that set Belma's life apart and made her "different." *Describe some of those differences.*

2. In spite of the differences in Belma's life, she credits her grandparents with giving her a "plumb line" (measuring stick) for building straight walls that gave her knowledge of right and healthy, wrong and abnormal. *What do you think this plumb line consisted of?*

3. *Can you identify a plumb line in your own life or history? Describe it (e.g., morality, a value system by which you live your life, an attitude or an outlook).*

4. *Examine the plumb line (morality, value system) on which you base truth one more time. Do you think this plumb line is trustworthy enough that you can build your life on it? If not, are you open to exchanging your plumb line for another? What would your new plumb line look like?*

5. *Examine your life against your plumb line again, and take some time to identify any areas in your life that need "straightening." Share it with someone else.*

CHAPTER 4: IN THE CLUTCHES OF A MONSTER

"Even though I walk through the darkest valley, I will fear no evil, for you are with me; your rod and your staff, they comfort me." (Psalm 23:4, NIV)

1. Twice in this chapter we see a victim of a bully finally pushing back in an effort to protect a beloved person from being ripped away from them—Oma at the threat of losing Belma to the customs guards, and Belma when Ingeborg tried to take her precious letters from her. On both

occasions the fury they displayed, born out of love and anger, caused a bully to back down. *Discuss the type of love that would place oneself in harm's way in order to protect another.*

2. *Do you think Oma and Opa's inability to protect Belma from her mother stemmed from the love and trust they still had for Ingeborg, from their fear of the authorities and the law, or from something else?*

3. Many people and institutions ignored or turned their backs on aiding Belma—a helpless child. *Has society changed today from what it was in the early 70s? How or how not?*

4. *Can you think of any other person or people group that has suffered in a similar way to Belma? How has society responded to them? In light of this chapter, how will you respond?*

5. Belma recalls her mother, saying, "She tried to destroy any sense of value in me," and later states that "A spiritual enemy was trying to destroy me through my mother." Jesus said, "The thief comes only to steal and kill and destroy; I have come that they may have life, and have it to the full" (John 10:10, NIV). *Contrast Belma's life with Oma versus her life with Ingeborg. Would you agree that an outside entity was influencing Ingeborg and persecuting Belma? Why or why not?*

6. Belma states, "I owned one precious thing—my long wavy hair down to my waist. My identity was wrapped up in it." *Identify something precious to you that sums up or acts as a container for your identity. If someone took it from you, how would you react? How would you recover?*

7. Belma releases hope with the statements, "many who have suffered the way I did do not recover, but there is a way," and "I can describe [situations] now without emotional pain." *Can you imagine your life free from the emotional pain of your past? Why or why not?*

CHAPTER 5: ESCAPE FROM HELL

"'For I know the plan I have for you,' declares the LORD, 'plans to prosper you and not to harm you, plans to give you hope and a future.'" (Jeremiah 29:11, NIV)

1. In this chapter we see Belma "coming of age." She no longer has to be under Ingeborg's authority. As she prepares to move out she receives impressions like "Don't take anything today." *Can you recall an impression that kept you from harm? Where do you think this impression came from?*

2. Belma made some significant life choices. One was to leave her mother's house, for her sanity and her life. Another was to stay away from anything that could derail her from her goals. *Do you have any goals you are working toward? Are there any life choices that you have made, or need to make, to help you reach your goals?*

3. While staying at Donna's house, Belma said, "As hard as it was to give up a nice, warm bed, the alternative was unacceptable," and so she became homeless. *Describe a situation that may be more unbearable than living on the street. How does this relate to your view of homeless people?*

4. *Can you see or describe strengths or values (plumb line) being built into Belma's psyche leading up to and during her time of homelessness?*

5. In this chapter Donna's character transforms from the concerned friend to "completely stoned and oblivious." *Discuss how people change through substance abuse and unhealthy relationships.*

6. *Contrast Belma's "every kind word and gesture pierced my heart" with Donna's oblivion. Why is it that some people can be so grateful with so little while others seem to throw away their riches and waste their potential?*

7. To Belma, Mike was a picture of the role God intended for dads. This was healing to her heart. *Has anyone mirrored the role of a healthy dad to you? Describe what you saw in him and how it has affected you in a positive way.*

8. With respect to First Nations people, Belma concludes with the reminiscence that "because we've shared similar pain in our hearts, I am able to understand them." *Describe the advantages that suffering can give us in our relationship with others.*

9. It is historically documented through thousands of interview hours from the Truth and Reconciliation events of 2008 to June 2015 that many First Nations people alive today suffered the same kinds of abuse, some at the same intensity, as Belma. One striking difference is that because Belma was allowed to stay with her grandparents until eight years of age, she retained a plumb line for normalcy and was able to keep and converse in her native tongue with her mother, difficult as their communication may have been. For some of our First Nations people, being taken away so early in life resulted in the loss of their ability to communicate with relatives at home and the loss of a plumb line regarding what is normal, since "normal" no longer existed around them. *Discuss how the additional fallout of loss of language and the ability to identify what is normal affect an individual. How do you think this could affect the larger community of First Nations? How is this now affecting the greater community of Canada?*

Recommended Reading on First Nations

- *Ojibway Tales*. Basil Johnston. Bison Books; reprint edition, October 1, 1993.
- *One Church Many Tribes*. Richard Twiss. Gospel Light Publications, August 8, 2000.
- *Victims of Progress*. Rowman & Littlefield Publishers; sixth edition, August 14, 2014.
- *Introduction to First Nations Ministry: Centre for Pentecostal Theology Native North American Contextualization*. Cheryl Bear-Barnetson. Cherohala Press, October 9, 2013.
- *The Honour Drum*. Cheryl Bear. Illustrated by Tim Huff. Castle Quay Books, 2016.
- For stories from residential school survivors or to get a copy of the video *Our Stories...Our Strength*, go to http://wherearethechildren.ca/en/stories/ and www.shareyourtruth.ca. The incidents in this book and in the

stories contain subject matter that may be disturbing to some viewers, particularly *survivors of the residential school system.* If you are in Canada, please call the Health Canada 24-hour National Survivors Crisis Line at 1–866–925–4419 if you need assistance.

CHAPTER 6: FROM RUNAWAY TO RUNWAY

"Do not conform to the pattern of this world, but be transformed by the renewing of your mind. Then you will be able to test and approve what God's will is—his good, pleasing and perfect will."
(Romans 12:2, NIV)

1. Belma and Lorne describe a hollowness or emptiness that Belma attempted to fill with marriage and a career. But these substitutions just underlined how deep the ache in her heart was. Belma says the emptiness "grew teeth" and "became a black hole." *Have you experienced that kind of "black hole" before? If so, how would you describe it?*

2. Belma mentions a "dark side to these material blessings" in reference to the nice clothes, the fussing over makeup, pretty pictures and nice paycheque—all which seem rather harmless. *How would you describe the "dark side"?*

3. Belma remembers feeling like a princess in the presence of her father and refers to having missed a mother to fuss over her. *Have you ever had a time in your life when you felt like royalty? What or who made you feel that way? Did the feeling last? Why or why not?*

4. Belma did everything she knew to overcome the void in her life due to a lack of parents. *Describe ways in which you or people you know have tried to fill a void. Did it work?*

5. Belma walked away from an easy $40,000 (40k in 1983 would be $181,000 now) because she refused to sell her body. *Where do you think she found the strength to do that? Would you be able to do the same?*

6. *How much value do you place on money and material things versus the well-being of your soul?*

CHAPTER 7: BREAKING DOWN THE WALLS

"And they cried out in a loud voice: 'Salvation belongs to our God, who sits on the throne, and to the Lamb.'" **(Revelation 7:10, NIV)**

1. After the Lord answered Belma's question about why He didn't do something she expected Him to do, she said, "I accepted what He said and was satisfied." *What do you think of this statement?*

2. Even though Belma had given her life over to Christ, unresolved issues from her past left her angry, hurt and alone. God reached out to her through a painting and the kindness of an artist. *Have you ever encountered God through the arts? Share your experience.*

3. Share an experience when you felt prompted to reach out to someone or when someone reached out to you in a way that felt miraculous.

4. "Don't go to the phone; go to the throne!" *Would you agree?*

5. Belma said, "I learned the dance of lament and the dance of grief." *Have you ever considered that your expression of negative emotions can be poured out as worship before the throne, whether in dance, art, music or some other creative means?*

6. *Talk about the value of movement as a form of therapy.*

CHAPTER 8: SURPRISING GOD ENCOUNTERS

"And I will show wonders in the heavens above and signs on the earth below." **(Acts 2:19, ESV)**

1. When God did not move in the way Belma expected, she took the situation back to Him in prayer. "I don't want you to tell Me when to

move. I want to be the One who inspires you to move." *Contrast God's desire to inspire us to move with us begging God to move at our call.*

2. When Belma received God's answer (see above question) she was satisfied and accepted it. Contrast the differences between someone who hears God's voice and applies it and one who hears His voice but continues to doubt or question.

3. Belma's statement that unresolved issues continued to plague her even after she came to Christ, suggests we still need to see the work of healing completed in our lives. *Discuss some of the miracles that God did in this chapter to bring about that healing, and how this affected you.*

4. In spite of her anger at God for allowing her to experience such severe trauma, she always talked about it to God. "Don't go to the phone, go the throne!" became her motto. *How do you deal with crisis when it comes? Do you run to God, or away from him?*

5. Belma found she could dance out her laments, anger, pain and grief the same way that King David, the psalmist, wrote and sang out his. *How do you release your pain? Have you ever considered that you could offer it up as a worship offering through an art form such as dance, or painting?*

6. Belma invited the Holy Spirit to be her best friend, but was afraid. "Come in the morning...," she said. *Why do you think Belma was afraid? What is your inward response to Belma's prayer, and what happened afterwards?*

7. God reached into Belma's life through a painting and the hug of a child. *Describe an instance when God reached into your life through art, or an act of kindness?*

8. Comment on Belma's statement concerning the desire for a spouse: "We have to surrender that desire to Him and be satisfied with Him alone." *How has this choice to be satisfied opened doors for her?*

CHAPTER 9: COMMISSIONED

"My presence will go with you." (Exodus 33:14, ESV)

1. Romans 12:1 says, "Present your bodies as a living sacrifice, holy and acceptable to God, which is your spiritual worship" (ESV). It gives us understanding that a body/spirit connection happens when we serve the Lord with our bodies. *Think of some ways you might worship the Lord this week with your body and take the time to do it!*

2. It had never occurred to Belma that her expression of love to Jesus could be categorized as dance. In fact, many good-hearted people have condemned dance as evil in the last few centuries, especially in westernized churches. *What do you think the difference was between Belma's expression of love to Jesus compared to her understanding of dance?*

3. Belma did not know she was in training for ministry. She simply pursued the Lord, expressing her love for Him in the way that was most natural to her. *Do you feel His presence more in some activities than in others? Do you do some alone, or in private?*

4. Somehow the Lord looked through all the dancers in the crowd to find and commission Belma for a ministry He had designed for her. *Share a time when it seemed as if the Lord looked through the crowd and found you.*

5. "In an instant I graduated from the closet to the stage because God had commissioned me." *Why do you think it was important for Belma to develop in private what the Lord wanted her to release publicly?*

6. Some people may never stand on a stage, but this chapter shows us that what we do in private is of value to the Lord. *Discuss the importance of developing your own private history with the Lord.*

7. *If you haven't already done so, take some time this week to consider how you might develop a private history with God. You may wish to make a*

timeline of your life and mark on it "God encounters," or answered prayers as well as significant life events. Are there any traditions you want to mark with Him (e.g., holidays or anniversaries, giving of thanks, etc.)? Is there a love language you want to develop with Him? For Belma it was movement. For you it may be taking a long walk, being quiet in His presence, listening to beautiful music, studying or meditating on Scripture. Make it a point to include some of these activities in your everyday life. Record some of your experiences and stand back and be amazed in a year's time.

CHAPTER 10: LEARNING TO FOLLOW

"All these blessings will come on you and accompany you if you obey the Lord your God." (Deuteronomy 28:2, NIV)

1. This chapter opens with God asking Belma to teach children how to pray. *Did these instructions surprise you? Why or why not?*

2. God gave each child in Belma's prayer group a spiritual vision. On one occasion, He opened their ears and eyes to the music and dance of Heaven, which they then re-enacted in the flesh. *Discuss the Scriptures "for the kingdom of heaven belongs to such as these" (Matthew 19:4, NIV, referring to a child), and "Suffer little children, and forbid them not, to come unto me: for of such is the kingdom of heaven" (Matthew 19:14, KJV). What do you think is meant by the statement, "for the kingdom of heaven [or reign of God] belongs to such as these"?*

3. When a father saw his son dancing so freely, he was moved to tears and said, "I'm trying to imagine what it's like to be so free and move like this but I'm so bound up I can't do it. Can somebody here please help me?" *Can you relate to this father's statement? Do you see freedom as a possibility?*

4. Belma states that this booking is what launched her ministry. *What does this tell you about people and the need to live a life of emotional freedom?*

5. Belma put together strict rules for her dance team, which were honoured by both the children and parents. *Why do you think these rules were necessary?*

6. In the next scene, we are confronted with a little girl who unintention-ally broke the rules, but God vouched for her and asked Belma to make an exception and put her into the dance. *What does this speak to you about the character of God?*

7. God asked Belma to lay down her teaching with the children, which was very difficult for her. *Has God ever asked you to do something that didn't make sense to you or was very difficult or painful?*

8. "They knew the Holy Spirit would empower them and minister through them if they did what they were supposed to do." *Discuss the importance of obedience in our personal walk with the Lord.*

9. Belma concludes this chapter with the statement "The incident reminded me how important it is for us to spend time alone with God because then we recognize His voice in critical times." *Share how God is teaching you to hear His voice. Can you recall a specific time when you heard Him clearly and it brought about success? Can you recall a time when you missed or disobeyed His voice and it cost you?*

10. Western thinking often forgets to address the internal heart issues of rebellion and submission. *Discuss how these principles are important for every age group, even children.*

11. *What do you believe the differences are between presentational dance, devotional dance and congregational dance?*

12. After Belma obeyed the Lord and taught the parents, whole families began to dance before the Lord. *Have you ever met a parent who has engaged with the Lord and their kids through dance? Is this something that you think should be nurtured in families? Why or why not?*

13. Belma recounts that after proper order had returned, the Lord allowed her to start instructing the children again. *What does this speak to you regarding God's heart for families and family order?*

CHAPTER 11: "MORE, LORD!"

"That you might be filled with all the fullness of God."
(Ephesians 3:19, ESV)

1. Belma talks of her time at the Toronto Airport Christian Fellowship and how it did not fit with her "Christian Reformed grid." *Has God ever gone outside your grid and done the unexpected? Describe your experience.*

2. "Whatever it takes to change me and make me more like You, I am open. I'm Yours." *Share why you think this could be an important prayer for the Lord to hear.*

3. Belma shares that receiving supernatural healing is not based on God's love for us but on what Jesus has already done for us. The underlying thought, of course, is that God loves us. *What is your reaction to this statement? Have you ever confused life's ups or downs with whether or not God loves you?*

4. God came to Belma through a dream and said, "You were healed... receive My love," indicating that there's a difference in God's mind between Belma receiving healing and Belma receiving God's love. *Share your thoughts on what those differences could look like to God.*

5. "I have dropped all expectations of what can or should happen in times I spend with Him," says Belma. She then talks about God not moving as often in physical manifestations as He had in the past and her feeling of being left out and on the outside. *Share an experience where you felt "left out" or "on the outside" and how it affected you.*

6. When Belma reached the children's area in the department store, she realized that God had indeed been moving powerfully inside her, healing her of emotional wounds and trauma from her first marriage. *Can you look at your life and discover God doing a hidden work that you couldn't see until it was complete?*

7. The emotional healing Belma received caused her to reach out to a woman who had hurt her deeply, and in so doing she was able to see God's restorative hand bring her nemesis to Christ. *Describe how partnering with God in ministry to Noreen may have brought great blessing to Belma. Is God directing you to reach out with kindness to someone who has hurt you?*

8. In Belma's healing journey, as she followed the desires of God's heart over her own, she found that her own walls of anger and bitterness collapsed and she was able to hear God's voice much more clearly. *Discuss the importance of hearing and obeying God's voice in our spiritual development.*

9. Belma recounts the thoughts of a woman to whom she had ministered in prayer. That woman now saw the ministry team as "doctors" and "nurses" through whom the chief physician, Jesus, was laying His healing hands on everyone. The mercy of God seemed to be poured out to everyone in Belma's story, whether they deserved it or not, and everyone associated with Jesus was given the opportunity to minister. *Share an experience of how you have been able to minister as a "doctor" or "nurse" on the chief physician's team.*

CHAPTER 12: FORGIVENESS AND HONOUR

"Honor your father and mother...that it go well with you." (Ephesians 6:2–3, ESV)

1. *Contrast Belma's impression that "Jesus wouldn't do that to His mother" with the lawyer's interpretation of the biblical values: "You have a right to your inheritance, and you need to come here and claim it." Discuss how Belma's following her Christian lawyer's advice might have set her on a different course than the one she chose.*

2. Ingeborg stole an inheritance but lost a husband, which resulted in her putting herself into a prison "of her own making," effectively judging her own self. *Contrast the heart of Jesus for mercy with our human need for justice. Discuss whether you think justice or mercy brings about the most change in people's lives.*

3. *Share an experience where you chose to extend mercy and wait for God's justice rather than taking matters into your own hands.*

4. In this chapter we see Jesus encouraging Belma to walk in mercy toward her mother so that both she and Ingeborg could receive God's justice, mercy and healing. Belma's obedience resulted in the salvation of others and deep inner healing for herself. Yet there are times when pressing charges against someone may be necessary to keep others out of harm's way, or even to protect one's self. This raises an important question: *When, if ever, is it appropriate to seek justice rather than mercy? Discuss your thoughts.*

5. When Belma applied to medical school she was made aware that God had another plan, but He told her that He would bless either path. He also let her know there would be a high sacrifice and cost on the path of ministry, but He promised that His presence would not leave her. Up to this point in the story, the emphasis has been on obedience. *Why do you think the Lord gave Belma a choice of vocation? What does this tell you about His heart?*

6. *Why do you think Belma chose ministry over medical school? Would this differ from your choice? Be careful not to "over compare" your story with Belma's, because God has His own unique plan for each life, including yours.*

7. Upon her mother's death, Belma found herself face to face with her mother's reality—some of it too painful to comprehend. Even though Belma had forgiven her mother, she still needed the input of a doctor and a counsellor to help her understand Ingeborg. The Lord was gracious to bring closure to every area concerning her mother, and at the end of her journey, Belma was able to release her mother with honour and gratefulness to God. *Is there any area of your family history that needs emotional closure? Remember, it took a year and a half before Belma could have a proper funeral for her mom. Where are you at on your journey of forgiveness?*

5. Scripture says, "'Honor your father and your mother' (this is the first commandment with a promise), 'that it may go well with you and that

you may live long in the land" (Ephesians 6:2–3, ESV). Belma honoured her mother in spite of incredible abuse. *Do you agree that as a result things went well with her? Why do you think this is the first and only commandment with a promise attached to it?*

CHAPTER 13: PREPARATION

"And they went forth...everywhere, the Lord working with them, and confirming the word with signs following." **(Mark 16:20, KJV)**

1. In this chapter we see the Lord giving Belma opportunity to grow as a dancer even though she did not have the resources to invest herself. *Take time to reflect: Are there areas in your life that need mentorship in order for you to grow in God's calling or design for your life? If so, take it to prayer and ask the Lord how to proceed.*

2. *If you are at a stage where you have received your practical training, is there any heart preparation you still need? Ask the Lord how to proceed. Make a plan, write it down and follow through.*

3. *Is there anybody or any group that you need to mentor? Ask the Lord how to proceed!*

4. One of Belma's teachers employed the "mock method" to show Belma what needed correcting. Belma says, "I had to perform with perfection or I would be mocked," but the training she received was "the best of the best." *Why do you think Belma was able to handle such rigorous training emotionally without her self-esteem collapsing? Would you be able to receive "mock" training? Why or why not?*

5. After receiving dreams of a dance video, Belma asked the Lord about it. He replied, "When are you starting the video?" She responded, "I thought You were doing it." Apparently not! *Is there something that the Lord has asked you to do that you have put off doing for lack of finances or for not knowing what to do? Have you taken any steps to obey Him? Why or why not?*

6. When Belma realized that the ball was in her court to get the video going even though God was partnering with her, she was ready to sell all her furniture to accomplish it. *How far would you be willing to go to accomplish something God had asked you to do?*

7. Belma shares that "He provides, guides our steps and gives promotion." *How have you seen this at work in your own life?*

8. At the end of this chapter, God gave Belma a new assignment that made her nervous. *Has there ever been a task or responsibility God has called you to that seemed overwhelming? Share how He got you through it and what you learned as a result.*

CHAPTER 14: INTO ALL THE WORLD

"Look at the nations and watch—and be utterly amazed. For I am going to do something in your days that you would not believe, even if you were told." (Habakkuk 1:5, NIV)

1. Belma's pastor recognized what Belma did as dance but called it "worship" and in so doing was able to plant seeds that made his congregation curious and hungry for this new expression. *Have you ever had a time when you, or people you are associated with, were not able to receive what God wanted to do because of the language used? How were you able to break through the barriers in order to receive what He wanted to do?*

2. Belma received a vision she didn't understand and was afraid to share, but her pastor responded, "We prayed that if it was God's will, He would confirm it by having you call." *Have you ever been in a situation where your ability to follow through made all the difference for the people surrounding you, even though you may have been afraid?*

3. *Talk about colours in worship and how they communicate what God is doing or wanting to do.*

4. Belma was again faced with a situation where a dancer lost his "right" to perform, but God demanded that he be put in the dance. Belma was

a bit slow in obeying God, but in the end she did it, and God blessed her and the church. *What does this speak to you about God's heart for people? What does this speak to you about the importance of our hearts to God versus our outward performance?*

5. On the subject of Belma's ministry, her pastor said, "We don't just say it with our mouths, but we do it with our bodies." *Discuss the importance of using our bodies to demonstrate what is in our hearts.*

6. A woman in Germany had flashbacks and screamed, "I hate you!" Rather than shutting her down, Belma allowed ministry to happen and recognized the woman's exposure of her pain as an opportunity. *What could you see yourself doing in a similar situation? Would you feel rejected or burdened and prayerful for the lady in pain? Brainstorm different ways you could lovingly handle this situation to the benefit of all.*

7. Belma speaks of needing to repent from defensive and arrogant attitudes when dealing with churches that are afraid of the type of anointing she brings. As God gives her revelation, she is able to see what He is doing in spite of what they are doing, and He is using Belma to bring healing to their wounded hearts. *Have you ever been sent to a place where the people didn't want you initially but really needed what you had to offer? What was your reaction? What was their reaction toward you? How did God intervene?*

8. Belma was confronted with setback after setback in making her video, and it became such a hard thing that she dreaded getting out of bed in the morning. As she persisted, however, the Lord released miracle after miracle to allow the video to be made. *Think of a situation in the past where you needed a God-intervention to get through. What was the result after God showed up? Are you going through anything now that needs a God-intervention?*

9. Belma states that her source of transformation is in worship. Through worship God can fight our battles for us so we don't have to deal with circumstances ourselves. *Share the importance of engaging*

God in worship when confronted with what would seem to be spiritual warfare.

CHAPTER 15: MASTER CHOREOGRAPHER

"Who comforts us in all our troubles, so that we can comfort those in any trouble with the comfort we ourselves receive from God."
(2 Corinthians 1:4, NIV)

1. This chapter opens with dancers from four distinct cultures choreographing the same moves to the same songs without ever having dialogued. *Share any relevant experiences where it seemed the Holy Spirit operated as the master choreographer in your life.*

2. Belma does not see giftings blending as competition but as an opportunity for unity to release blessing. *Discuss the phrase "compete or complete." Why do you think this is an important principle to grasp?*

3. *Are there people in your life with whom you feel synergy in ministry? How might you complement them? How do they complement you?*

4. *What do you do when feelings of jealousy or competition arise? Are you secure enough to move past them and see the individual as someone who can make your team better?*

5. *Spend some time asking the master choreographer to speak to you about your value and what you can contribute on His team. Repent of any competitive or jealous tendencies and ask the Lord to give you a picture of Him directing His team, be it a dance team, a symphony or a sports team.*

6. *What was the "river of healing" in Belma's story, and how did it come to be? Can you think of any place in Scripture that speaks of a similar river? (HINT: see Ezekiel 47, Revelation 22 and John 7:38.) How can you access this river?*

7. *The Lord may have given you your own word picture that really helped you at a certain point in your life. Share it with the group.*

8. Belma speaks of Jesus taking a mantle off her and directing her elsewhere. *What do you think the mantle represents? Discuss how the Lord rewarded Belma's obedience not to go.*

9. *Reflect on your own life: is there a place or situation God is asking you to avoid? Can you release it to Him?*

10. *Take some time this week to seek the Lord and ask Him to show you a picture of His river of healing, whether it's in your imagination, out in nature or by a supernatural dream or vision. Ask Him the significance of the river for your own life, and find a way to release your burdens to the Lord (e.g., writing them on paper and letting them float downstream, placing them under a rock, etc.). Be prepared to share your experience in the next group session.*

CHAPTER 16: BLESSED

"The Spirit of the Sovereign LORD is on me, because the LORD has anointed me to proclaim good news to the poor. He has sent me to bind up the brokenhearted, to proclaim freedom for the captives and release from darkness for the prisoners, to proclaim the year of the LORD's favor." (Isaiah 61:1–2, NIV)

1. *Start with sharing your own experience with the Lord as you sought Him regarding the river of healing from last week's study.*

2. In this chapter it seems that the work of God comes full circle for Belma. She begins the chapter assuring us of God's promises for healing and then says, "I believe that the grace of God that flows through this ministry is rooted in the ability God gave me to forgive my mother." *Looking back through previous chapters, what were some of the things for which Ingeborg needed forgiveness? What did it cost Belma to truly forgive on an emotional level? How long did it take for the forgiveness to be complete?*

3. *Reflect on your own life. Are there any people that are in need of your forgiveness? Where do you think you are on your own journey to forgive them?*

4. Belma credits God with the ability to forgive her mother. Alexander Pope once wrote, "To err is human, to forgive divine." *Ask the Holy Spirit to come and give you the strength and ability you need to forgive others on every level. Wait in His presence to see if He releases any instructions, and ask Him for His peace and courage.*

5. Belma exclaims that God has provided blessings wherever she goes and that she is treated like royalty. *Reflect on past chapters where Belma longed to be fussed over and to feel like a princess in her daddy's presence. What changed for her?*

6. It is interesting to note that Jesus promises us that "Everyone who has left houses or brothers or sisters or father or mother or wife or children or fields for my sake will receive a hundred times as much" (Matthew 19:29, NIV). In Belma's story, she found just that. She explains, "At whatever church God sends me to, the pastor and his wife become my family." *In light of this Scripture, and by her own admission, discuss how God restored Belma's inheritance and family.*

7. Belma always asks the pastor and leadership of the church about their vision so she can support what God is already doing. *Discuss why this could be an important and necessary step in establishing a relationship with other ministries and churches.*

8. Belma speaks of God allowing her to "play"—something she did not get a chance to do under Ingeborg. *How does this affect your view of God as Master or Father?*

9. *Do you agree with Belma's comment that a dancer's appropriate clothes contribute to "the ability of people to connect with God"? Share ideas how to keep the dance sacred so the Lord can be the focus.*

10. In Belma's ministry it seems that people of all ages and races and both genders can identify with the same hunger for intimacy with the Lord. *Discuss the comment "The men were so unaffected by my femininity that they could confess their deepest sins in my presence," in light of the Scripture, "There is neither Jew nor Greek, there is neither slave nor free,*

there is no male and female, for you are all one in Christ Jesus" (Galatians 3:28, ESV).

CHAPTER 17: WHERE THE RIVER FLOWS / PREFACE

"Where the river flows everything will live." (Ezekiel 47:9, NIV)

1. Belma makes the statement in the preface that "God is a great steward, wasting nothing of our pain." This agrees with Psalm 56:8, which states, "You keep track of all my sorrows. You have collected all my tears in your bottle. You have recorded each one in your book" (NLT). *What are some of your sorrows that God has promised to remember? What are the tears in your bottle? Have you seen Him bring good out of them, or are you still trusting Him for that?*

2. Belma's horrific childhood makes her the perfect person to minister to Canada's most oppressed people group. *Share how you've been able either to comfort others with the comfort you have received or to receive comfort from someone who has been through similar circumstances to your own: "who comforts us in all our troubles, so that we can comfort those in any trouble with the comfort we ourselves receive from God" (2 Corinthians 1:4, NIV).*

3. The preface sheds light on a problem that is not restricted to Canada but also extends to the United States, regarding the damage that the Indian Act enacted upon Indigenous people. *Take some time to reflect and share how the phrase quoted by an official, "Kill the Indian in the child," might have enabled abusers or caused damage in a child's self-esteem.*

4. *With 80,000 survivors still living, and the last residential school not closing until 1996, discuss the mindset that says, "Why are we discussing problems that happened hundreds of years ago?" Armed with more factual information, how has this information affected you?*

5. *What do you believe the value is in observing protocol with First Nations and other cultural groups before sharing the gospel? What does the fact*

that God lined up the protocol for Belma to minister to First Nations tell you about His heart for First Nations people and cultures?

6. Belma was presented with an eagle feather from two chiefs—a very high honour that communicated their appreciation and acceptance of her ministry. *Contrast this action with the feelings that First Nations People often carry toward religious institutions. What made the difference?*

7. In this chapter a man named Jerry enters the story. He was unwittingly used by the government to inflict harm upon a people group he grew to love and appreciate. Jerry is now doing all he can to make restitution and has been used by the Lord to minister to many, yet it is a debt he will never be able to repay. *Discuss Jerry's felt need to make restitution and how it may fit into God's plan. (HINT: contrast Old Testament—Psalm 79:12, Exodus 22:1 and Proverbs 6:31—with the New Testament—Ephesians 4:28.) Discuss the need for Jerry to find personal forgiveness.*

8. This book ends with the statement "It was only possible *because God was there*," referring not only to the healing work of God but to the full life of love and belonging that Belma is experiencing. *Reflect on and share the difference God has made in your own life. Consider writing a five- to ten-minute presentation of your story. Come back to your group for one last meeting where everyone can share and join in celebration together.*

Now that you have read Belma's story, consider inviting God into the centre of your story in a greater, more personal way.

Suggested Prayer

Heavenly Father, Belma's story gives me hope that my sorrows can also be turned into laughter and that they can be used to bring comfort and peace to someone else. Please step onto centre stage in my heart and teach me how to live as Belma lived: learning to forgive, to hear Your voice and to walk with You wherever You call me. Help me to release all those who have hurt me. Please forgive me for any ways in which I have hurt You, myself or others. I turn my sorrows, my anger and my bitterness over to You now.

Please make something beautiful from my life. I receive all that Jesus has done for me in forgiving my sins by taking my punishment through dying on a cross. Amen.

About the Author

B elma Vardy, a Bible college graduate and former actress/model, was born in Toronto, Canada, but raised by her grandparents in Berlin, Germany. She is an ordained minister with Global Christian Ministry Forum and serves her church community in Mississauga. Since 1994, Belma has served on the Catch the Fire Toronto (TACF) ministry team, and since 1995, she has worked with leaders and elders in Inuit, Métis and First Nations communities to bring a ministry of freedom through artistic expression of their culture.

For 31 years, Belma has ministered to people through dance and therapeutic movement with gentleness and dedication, bringing them into deeper intimacy with God and freedom in worship through movement. A seasoned public speaker, she has taught and presented throughout Canada, the United States, Europe, South Africa, Asia, United Kingdom, South America, the Islands and the Arctic. Due to her special love for children she was appointed the coordinator for the International Christian Dance Fellowship's (ICDF) Network for Children's Dance, and she is grateful that Roz Hancock now serves alongside her as joint coordinator. Belma also served for 7 years as the national coordinator representing Canada for adult worship dance with the Christian Dance Fellowship of Canada, under the umbrella of ICDF.

Belma has been made appearances on 100 *Huntley Street*, *Circle Square Discovery*, *Catch the Fire* (television and radio programs), and the Miracle Channel. Parts of her testimony are published in Dr. Guy Chevreau's *Catch the Fire* and *Pray with Fire*.

Both the videos and this book that Belma has done are projects under Imago (www.imago-arts.org). All who wish to make a tax deductible donation toward a project, such as the translation of *Because God Was There*, can make cheques payable to "The Freedom Project" and forward them to Belma Vardy, P.O. Box 20104, 2211 Brant St., Burlington, Ontario, Canada L7P OA4.

Celebration of Dance

MISSION STATEMENT

*The vision of Celebration of Dance
is to foster intimacy with God
on both an individual and corporate level,
through teaching and encouragement of
children, youth and adults
to express their hearts in
pure and wholesome worship
through dance and movement.*

*To achieve this vision, Celebration of Dance
has produced videos for youth
and children on various themes using the arts:
music, drama, praise and worship dance—
to bring reconciliation and healing
to hearts and nations.*

*Testimonies abound of children who have come
into a living relationship with Jesus Christ
through these videos.*

RESOURCES

Please visit www.celebrationofdance.com to order
or contact us at customercare@celebrationofdance.com

TO CONTACT BELMA VARDY

905–336–1499
belmavardy@celebrationofdance.com
P.O. Box 20104, 2211 Brant St., Burlington,
Ontario, Canada L7P OA4
www.becausegodwasthere.com
info@becausegodwasthere.com

Action Songs for Worship 1

DVD or Download

Action Songs for Worship 2

DVD or Download

Action Songs for Worship 3

DVD or Download

Action Songs for Worship 4

DVD or Download

Dancing with God: Amazed

DVD or Download

Dance Into Battle

DVD or Download

Breakout: Freedom in the Streets

DVD or Download

Devotional Dance Workshop

DVD or Download

Let's Dance

DVD or Download

I Lift Your Name on High

DVD or Download

River of Healing

DVD or Download

Riviére de Guerison

DVD or Download

Now Is the Time

DVD or Download

Biblical Basis for the Celebration of Dance

DVD or Download

Celebration of Dance Music Songbook

Celebration of Dance Music CD

The Honour Drum is a uniquely envisioned and crafted project shared between two Canadian friends—an Indigenous woman from the West Coast and a non-Indigenous man from Ontario—to reach children, families and classrooms across Canada and around the world with a message of great beauty and truth that should not be ignored. This vibrant book is an important starting place for learning and insight that is vital and, for many people of all ages, overdue. *The Honour Drum* is a love letter to the Indigenous people of Canada and a humble bow to Indigenous cultures around the world.

It's Hard Not to Stare encourages children to look at their world through the lens of compassion and understanding, rather than assumption, judgment or fear. Tim Huff believes this approach will impact the way we care for and befriend people in our communities and beyond, and that when we nurture compassion in a child in one area of life, the potential is great that this goodness will spill over into all other areas. Tim addresses issues related to disabilities in tender and truthful prose, along with bright and courageous child-friendly illustrations.

Bent Hope was born out of Tim Huff's first twenty years of unique and extensive work among homeless and street involved youth and adults, in one of North America's largest urban centres—Toronto, Canada. *Bent Hope* is a collection of thoughtful narratives birthed beneath crumbling bridges and in the hidden alcoves of darkened alleyways after midnight. These gripping true-life stories surface quietly from unforgiving corridors of fear, hurt and uncertainty—and unexpectedly and supernaturally transform them into fascinating places of intimacy and godly anticipation.

"Tim is a true champion for justice. He also happens to be a street poet, a missional activist, and a wide-eyed mystic who is able to discern the traces of God in the strangest of places. This book is an enticing exploration of redemptive grace-in-action on the streets of Toronto."—Alan Hirsch, author of *The Forgotten Ways*

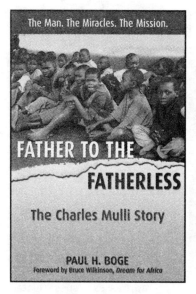

Father to the Fatherless is the true story of a man whose life begins in desperate poverty, moves to riches, and finally servanthood, where he becomes a real-life demonstration of selfless love and sacrifice that challenges us to evaluate the cost of giving up all to God in the service of others.

Six-year-old Charles Mulli wakes up in his Kenyan hut to discover his parents have abandoned him. Forced to beg in search of food, Charles scrapes out a meagre existence. As a teenager, Charles is invited by a friend to a crusade where he commits his life to Christ. That act begins a unique adventure of faith, miracles, and a passion for reaching street children. After years of struggle, Charles experiences unprecedented success. He finds a wonderful wife, raises a family, excels in business to such a degree that he creates an empire that is noticed by the President of Kenya. Then, convicted by God to give away all his possessions, Charles sells everything to pursue his passion of rescuing street children from the slums of Kenya. He battles against corrupt religious establishments, supernatural enemies, and intense financial pressures to bring hope to those whose lives reflect his own childhood.

"Riveting, invigorating, poignant and very funny. This book is for anyone who is or is becoming a leader."—Mark Buchanan, author of *The Rest of God*

"An inspiring collection of stories from eight uniquely called and gifted leaders!"—Liz Curtis Higgs, best-selling author of *The Girl's Still Got It*

"Not your typical leadership book. It's a keeper."—Jim Cantelon, author and host of Jim Cantelon Today

"The stories in this book are excellent examples of Christian leadership and deserve our full attention."—Preston Manning, founder of the Manning Centre